"Why does God spare one house on a street hit by a tornado but not the others? Why does God allow innocent children to die or save one poor soul from cancer, but not another? Brandon Ambrosino, a new and exciting theological voice, shows that these are not inscrutable mysteries to be accepted, but confused questions and blasphemous images of God. Against this bankrupt theology, [Ambrosino] offers a radically new conception of God which honors God's love and human dignity, and seriously engages the beautiful risk of life—a risk for both God and us."

—John D. Caputo, Thomas J. Watson professor emeritus of religion, Syracuse University, David R. Cook professor emeritus of philosophy, Villanova University

"Brandon Ambrosino's book is a pleasure to read. And it's not just his accessible writing and probing insights. It's also the vision of God he sets forth, often as a rejoinder to unhelpful visions of the divine. This is the kind of book I'll give a thoughtful person asking tough questions and seeking loving and hopeful answers."

—Thomas Jay Oord, author of *God Can't: How to Believe in God* and *Love after Tragedy, Abuse, and Other Evils*

"Ambrosino offers a bold and deeply personal challenge to traditional theologies that portray God as micromanaging human suffering. Instead of defending an all-controlling deity who permits or orchestrates disaster, this book introduces us to a God who is intimately entangled in our world's pain, creatively responding to it alongside us and guiding us—through deep sorrow—toward radical hope. This is the God we need in our world today."

— Ish Ruiz, PhD, assistant professor of Latinx & Queer decolonial theology, coordinator of the Latinx roundtable at CLGS

"Brandon Ambrosino invites us to acknowledge that this disorderly and often painful world defies our systematized theologizing. If God saved a presidential candidate from assassination, why not the firefighter who did die? If God controls everything, why punish a world that's gone wrong? If God is free to forgive, why must Jesus die? In response to such questions Ambrosino reads biblical texts with a discomfiting closeness, revealing that God becomes God in relationship with and among us, 'a god whose godness consists precisely in his loving.'"

— Greg Carey, PhD, professor of New Testament, Lancaster Theological Seminary

"In his accessible and conversational style, Brandon Ambrosino invites readers to explore profound questions about suffering and divine will. Does God care about our pain? Is suffering part of God's plan? Drawing from contemporary theology—particularly theopoetics—alongside ethics and science, Ambrosino offers illuminating insights on these challenging questions. His journey through tragedy and meaning culminates in a powerful observation: 'hope for the world is not possible unless we first acknowledge that the world is a place worth hoping for.' Dr. Ambrosino's writing is clear, engaging, and thoughtful, making complex theological concepts accessible to readers of all ages. Using suffering as a starting point, the book ultimately asks us to examine what kind of God we believe in. This exploration proves especially valuable in our current era, where suffering and hope intertwine amid global uncertainty and change."

— Ilia Delio, OSF, Josephine C. Connelly endowed chair in theology, Villanova University

"Brandon Ambrosino does theology that makes me literally shout with joy from my desk chair. That might seem like a weird endorsement for a book about suffering, but trust me: He's the writer to take with you into the darkest places."

—Jessica Mesman, senior editor, *The Christian Century*

"Brandon Ambrosino is one of my favorite thinkers. His writing never fails to fascinate, and he explores the topics of suffering and hope with depth, clarity, and compassion. *Is It God's Will?* is a welcome antidote to the cynicism of the world around us."

— David Robson, author of *The Intelligence Trap*, *The Expectation Effect* and *The Laws of Connection*

"In *Is It God's Will?*, Ambrosino sits with the uncomfortable, down in the basement of theology, as he calls it. And he invites his readers to go down there with him. To ask the difficult questions, even if the answers remain incomplete and unsatisfying. To struggle with how to even ask the question. To think about what happens when God happens in this world that is far from perfect, and in which, against all odds, good things also happen. This is innovative theology with style, both delightful to read and rich food for thought."

—Stefanie Knauss, professor of constructive theology, theology and religious studies, Villanova University

Is It God's Will?

Is It God's Will?

Making Sense of Tragedy, Luck, and
Hope in a World Gone Wrong

Brandon Ambrosino

Some of this book's text was previously published in *The Christian Century*, especially the article, "Did God Save Donald Trump's Life?" which appeared in the September 2024 issue.

Some of this book's text, especially Chapter 5, "Hope in a World Gone Wrong," appeared in the author's dissertation, "Flamingos, Flirts, and Flea Markets: Theo-Ethical Notes on Camp" (submitted April 2024, Department of Theology and Religious Studies at Villanova University).

Morehouse Publishing
19 East 34th Street
New York, NY 10016

Morehouse Publishing is an imprint of Church Publishing Incorporated.

Cover design by David Baldeosingh Rotstein
Typeset by Stefan Killen

ISBN 978-1-64065-841-7 (hardcover)
ISBN 978-1-64065-842-4 (eBook)

Library of Congress Control Number: 2025934362

To Rusty, Violet, and Agnes,

God is with you—and he is with Daddy.
I love you.

Table of Contents

"God is our last hope because
we are God's first love."

—JÜRGEN MOLTMANN

Introduction

The world seems to have gone very wrong recently. There are the big goings-wrong, like the breakdown of global relations, wars in the Middle East and Sudan, and climate disasters. The United States seems poised on the edge of disintegration while other major world powers coyly mention nuclear war. Longtime global partnerships risk dissolution, while warring factions within the United States seem to be gaining momentum, audacity, and legitimation. Anxieties feel to be at an all-time high. Covid showed us the inadequacies both of our healthcare system and our social bonds: masks, vaccines, and social distancing were brandied about as nothing but weapons in a longstanding culture war. And while Covid did not precipitate the public's distrust of institutions, to many people it offered definitive proof that they could no longer trust Big Government, Big Pharm, and Big News. Perhaps this is why gun ownership is on the rise: Many people feel they must take their family's safety into their own hands. But more guns only add to our collective sense of anxiety: in a country with more guns than people, any old place—shopping mall, concert venue, house of worship—becomes the next location with a Wikipedia entry. Add to this list concerns about the rapid development of AI, outrageous inflation rates, and the spiraling costs of basic healthcare, and it becomes clear that our general sense of anxiety seems to be grounded in reality.

There also smaller goings-wrong—smaller in the sense of local, close to home. These are the things that go wrong in our personal lives: cancer diagnoses, car wrecks, layoffs, foreclosures.

As I was driving back to Delaware from Maine last summer, I received a text message that the forty-four-year-old father of our goddaughters had suddenly died of a heart attack. My husband, Andy, and I traveled straightaway to Florida to be with the girls and their mother, Rusty. Two days later, we were at a kitchen table struggling to find words to tell the two-and-a-half-year-old that her father wasn't coming home. "God just wanted to be with Daddy so much," said their mother, "that he took him to heaven." My theological sensibilities suggested I intervene, but my friend instincts told me to remain quiet, and reminded me that what was important was for this mother and daughter to begin their journey to healing.

A few weeks earlier, my friend experienced a painful miscarriage. As I struggled to comfort her husband, Dan, he simply shrugged and said, "The baby didn't want to be in there. He made his choice." Same shudder, same instincts.

My friends were using different vocabularies—Rusty's was explicitly theological, and Dan's wasn't. But they were essentially making similar claims: The tragedy they experienced wasn't really a tragedy; it was a decision. It didn't just happen; someone was pulling the strings. Although these claims troubled me, I could tell they brought my friends some comfort. That, after all, is one of the tasks of good theology (that is, to comfort the afflicted).

Still, I couldn't help but wonder what would happen if my goddaughter were to grow up believing that God took her dad because he wanted to be with him. Does that mean God is selfish? Doesn't God know that Carl's family also wants to be with him? Did God send the heart attack to get him to heaven quickly? Could he not have found a less horrific way to do it? Could he have given Rusty some advanced notice? Or maybe my goddaughter will start to wonder why God doesn't take all of us to heaven right now—does he not love us as much as he loves Carl? Are these actually comforting thoughts?

And what about Dan's reasoning: that the babies chose not to be with him and his wife? Did this put his mind at peace? I wondered if he thought the same thing about the losses that my husband, Andy, and I suffered. For three years, we pursued parenthood via IVF. With the help of a family member, who generously volunteered to be our gestational carrier, we struggled to create new life. During our journey, we transferred three embryos—none of which survived. The last failure was exceptionally distressing. A few weeks after being told we were pregnant, we discovered our carrier had a blighted ovum: an embryo sac was growing, but there was no baby inside of it. As the three of us stared at the ultrasound monitor, each dealing with the third loss in our own way, we realized our dreams were once again being deferred. Should we comfort ourselves like Dan did, convincing ourselves that all three embryos made a choice not to become our child?

Every day, we find ourselves in the position that Rusty and Dan were in: Forced to come to terms with very bad news, we grope for an explanation until we find the one that feels the least bad. For thousands of years, people of faith have engaged in this activity, and have often roped God into the conversation at an early stage. So, for instance, God, we argue, is the one who calls the shots, who makes the decisions, who . . . sends the heart attack?

But this is at odds with the Christian conviction that God is love, that God is for us, with us, crazy about us. This isn't some sappy claim, that God is pursuing us like he is some big city lawyer forced to unexpectedly spend his holiday in our quaint little Hallmark town. No, the love of God is eternal, constant, unwavering, piercing. It is what gives us life; it is the power by which we come to be, by which we are sustained in this life and beyond. It is God's YES to us—to who we are, both as we are and as we are becoming all that we might become. As soon as God speaks this YES, speaks his love, he becomes emotionally caught up with all that he is loving. This is the key; this is what makes God's love *love*: God issues to us his YES, and then waits to hear our response and is personally invested in our response. Not because he wants to know the answer so much as the answer-er. As Thomas Aquinas puts it, "The lover is not satisfied with a superficial apprehension of the beloved, but strives to gain an intimate knowledge of everything pertaining to the beloved."[1]

Love wants to learn about the beloved, to learn what and how and why he's feeling, to become familiar with his hopes and fears and fancies. "Love seeks the other," writes theologian Werner G. Jeanrond. "Love desires to relate to the other, to get to know the other, to admire the other, to experience the other's life, to spend time with the other. . . . Hence love *always includes emotion*, yet it is more than emotion."[2] To say that God is love is to say that the most important thing about God is God's emotional entanglement, his edge-of-his-seat enthrallment with all that is.

So where does this leave us? Christians believe that God is intimately related to this world, to everything that happens in this world. But how we can talk meaningfully, how can we talk honestly about this relationship? I think Christianity suffers when we frame this relationship in terms of power—God causing a war, causing someone to die, making a mother miscarry, changing the trajectory of an assassin's bullet.

How, then, ought we think about God's relationship to our world, a world that continues to go wrong, to spin off course, to wound us daily?

We might not be able to construct an answer, as in *the* answer, as in *the one and only answer*. Anyone who's suffered knows on a gut level that this kind of answer doesn't exist. Suffering is unanswerable. By its very nature, suffering eludes us, steals away our words, mocks us as we try to get our heads around it. Suffering is—if we can make up a word, and we'd better be OK with making up words if we're going to do theology—*unsystematizable.* There is no system, theological or otherwise, within which suffering makes sense. Suffering is a disruption of meaning. It is, in fact, antimeaning. It interrupts, throws out of whack the world as we like to think of it, as we want it to be, as we expect it to be. We cannot solve suffering, and attempting to do so only discounts the suffering and degrades the sufferers.

But while we can't make meaning out of suffering, we might be able to make meaning *from* suffering—that is, after the fact of suffering. To do this, we need to start with the fact of suffering. And to do this as Christians, we need to start with the fact of God's suffering. As Jürgen Moltmann says, the Christian God most fully reveals himself in the cross of Jesus, which is a real moment of real suffering.[3] We cannot "solve" this suffering by approaching God too systematically, by arguing, for instance, that God the Father was not present to the suffering of the Son as he hung on the cross. The Apostle Paul says that God was *in Christ* reconciling the world to himself (2 Cor. 5:19). There is no moment in Jesus's life when God is not actively embracing the world. Jesus *is* the activity of God. Jesus is both what God does in the world and how God does it. And what God does, according to the New Testament witness, is to allow himself to endure the sufferings of Calvary. Systematic theology cannot remove God from the cross; only God can save God, and that is precisely what God refuses to do.

If you had walked into one of my freshmen classrooms at Liberty University, my undergraduate alma mater, you would have thought we were doing math. You would have seen a blackboard covered in spiraling diagrams and complicated charts, and you would have heard the teacher wax eloquent about the distinctions between concepts like "preordained" and "foreordained." "This is you," he would say, pointing to a terrified girl in the front row and drawing a stick figure on the board, "at the moment of your salvation." He'd then draw a timeline below the figure. "Here is when *justification* happens. And here," he drew the same stick figure a little further down the timeline, "is when, God willing, your sanctification happens. And finally"—one more figure—"you reach the stage of glorification." These were the various stages, or tenses, of salvation.

This made sense to most of us. Salvation, we believed, was instantly received as a gift from God that was freely given so long as you did something to earn it, such as say a prayer. But the problem was that not everyone who had said that prayer truly *acted* saved. But we couldn't very well say they weren't saved because then that would mean our prayer thing didn't do the trick. So our teachers, resourceful as ever, undertook to explain systematically and grammatically that different aspects of salvation occurred at different times. This could explain how people who said the prayer could also be people who sinned badly: They were going to heaven, but they were as of yet unsanctified. The goal was fitting everything into one giant theological system where every part illuminated every other. This, I was taught, was systematic theology.

Even in those classrooms, I had a healthy allergy to systematic theology. It was too neat; too tidy; too easy to put together, like a TV stand from IKEA. Systematic theology constructs a *system* that makes sense of all its component parts, shows how they all fit together perfectly, snugly, soundly. For instance: "God loves humans so much that he gives us free will, and we can use it to choose to go to hell. Because hell is our free choice, we can still maintain that God is love." In this example, systematic theology shows us how God doesn't send people to hell even though he does. The system is coherent, consistent, and organized. The word "systematic," says Jason Wyman, "arose as the preferred term and approach to doing theology in the academy as theology sought to keep up with the systematization of other academic disciplines that grew in prominence, especially in the

Enlightenment."[4] Wyman quotes at length Paul Tillich, for whom the "tight circle" of systematic theology means that "every part is dependent on every other part."[5]

There is no doubt that many theologians, even those such as myself who criticize systematic theology, nevertheless employ its methods. In fact, many of us have great admiration for the many systematic theologians who inspire, educate, and challenge us; their fingerprints are all over our work (including this book!).

At the same time, I do, as I say, have a certain allergy to Systematic Theology, especially when it announces its presence via capital letters. This goes back to my days at Liberty University, where, while learning about The System, I came to realize that I myself did not have a place in it. I was unsystematic. And what is a systematic theologian to do with the unsystematic? Very simple: Bend or reform or break him until he fits into the system. There can be nothing outside the system. The integrity of the system depends on this claim. And so I wound up in a therapist's chair where, twice a week, he led me through psychological exercises aimed at helping me discover when and why I started to leave the system. To be gay within this system, I learned, was to be gay *with respect to the system*: You were either in open rebellion against God or on your way back to him. The system explains, constrains, interprets you, de-queers you, and in this way makes the uncomfortable *other* just one more cog in a machine. After years of being manipulated to fit into a theological system that made no room for me *as me*, I decided that being unsystematizable wasn't so bad. (In fact, it was by reading brilliant systematicians that I learned that God wanted me to be me *as me*. Which meant not me within someone else's system, but me within *God's*.)

The theology that I'm after in this book is constructive: We are going to journey honestly to sites of suffering and, with equal parts fear and audacity, attempt to speak the name of God. As John D. Caputo likes to say, there is an event that happens in the name of God, in the name *God*.[6] This event is not our conjuring-up or our imagining, not our doing. This event really happens *to us*. Is God this event? Answering the "is" question in respect to God is an obsession of many systematic theologians in both the academy and in our churches. I do not know what God is, but I believe that God *is* up to something in the world, and that in fact, this *being up to something* is the event that happens whenever we speak or hear the name God. God is whatever God is up to.

So rather than ask what God is, we are going to reflect on what happens when and where God happens, and also what happens when we happen in response to God's happening. Now, we might reply that God happens when and where we want God to happen, and that's not entirely wrong. But I'm interested in another God-happening, a happening that happens in ways we don't happen to expect. I'm talking about what Caputo calls the *insistence* of God. God insists upon us, and this insistence floods in on us when we come to our end, when we hit a brick wall, when we stare into the abyss of despair. In these moments of darkness, when our suffering is unbearable, when our world is collapsing around us, we discover ourselves being visited, being summoned, being called. To what?

To hope. And to do so in spite of the fact that there is no reason to hope.

To hope against hope is to confess the name of God from the depths of a hopeless world.

What, then, is the event that happens in the name of God? It is simply this: the provocation to hope.

ONE

Getting Comfortable in the Basement

Does God really call the shots?

"The world is disgracefully managed, one hardly knows to whom to complain."
—RONALD FIRBANK, *VAINGLORY*

In the summer of 2024, I learned how to do the theology of a presidential assassination attempt. During a July campaign rally in Butler County, Pennsylvania, eight rounds of gunfire rang out a little after 6:11 p.m., sending rallygoers and the Secret Service scrambling. During the commotion, two people were critically injured (although later released from the hospital). One person, Cameron Comperatore, former chief of the Buffalo Township Volunteer Fire Company, was killed. So was the would-be assassin, who was taken out by a sniper. President Trump was shot in his right ear. Before Secret Service agents could carry him offstage, Trump raised his right hand into the air and shouted, "Fight! Fight! Fight!" Perhaps a fittingly violent response to a shockingly violent moment.

For hours, we waited for answers: Who was the shooter? What were his motives? How did he get that close? How was President Trump? Would he need surgery? What about the victims in the hospital? Almost immediately, though, there was another answer making its way across various media: Trump is alive because God kept him alive. This claim was the ultimate, well, Trump card in the torturous culture wars that had for the past few decades been gathering momentum and rage. By saving Trump's life from an assassin's bullet, God had clearly announced which side he was on.

Just ask Franklin Graham, who, just before offering a prayer at Trump's second inauguration, addressed Trump in this way: "Mr. President, the last four years, there were times I'm sure you thought it was pretty dark, but look what God has done!" Moments later, Trump himself concurred. "Just a few months ago, in a beautiful field, an assassin's bullet ripped through my ear. But I felt then and believe even more so now that my life was saved for a reason. I was saved by God to make America great again."

Call it the Theology of a Presidential Assassination Attempt. It goes like this.

Step one: Start by believing that God is all powerful, is in control of everything that happens, and takes a special interest in US politics.

Step two: Remind yourself that God can override free will whenever God wants to or whenever it's in the divine interest to do so, like when it concerns US politics.

Step three: Convince yourself that God is capable of intervening in human affairs in a way that can determine the next president of the United States while simultaneously respecting the free will of the voters.

Step four: God was responsible for saving President Trump's life.

But before proceeding to step five, maybe we should take a moment and think about where we're headed. How exactly did God save Trump's life from a bullet? Did he[1] cause the former president to move his head just so? Did he send a wind to alter the trajectory of the bullet? Did he cause the would-be assassin to twitch just as he pulled the trigger of the gun? I suppose I'm overthinking it. After all, "God's ways are not our ways" (Isaiah 55:8), as Christians are fond of saying when coming to terms with suffering. I guess the Christian thing to do is set these questions aside and keep climbing the stairs until we feel satisfied with where we end up.

But there's another possibility. We might think about climbing the steps in the other direction, down to the basement. Be warned, though. It's creepy down there, and dark, and very cold. There are only a few lightbulbs hanging from overhead pipes. In the darkness of this underground space, uncomfortable questions are given voice, allowed to take up space, to breathe. Questions we wouldn't dare ask in the light of the morning room crawl across the cracking cement floor like scurrying centipedes.

And yet it is here in this dank, ominous basement where theology gets up to its most important work. After all, this is the structure that upholds the entire theological edifice we are occupying.

I'm using the metaphor of a basement to call attention to something that every theologian knows well: underneath the theological questions that we don't know how to answer are other theological questions that we don't even know how to ask.

So, for instance, if the living is room where we ask how exactly God moved Trump's head out of the way of the shooter's bullet, the basement is where we ask if God caused the bullet to end up in a firefighter's body. In polite company, we talk about God miraculously saving Trump; in the basement, we awkwardly ask why God wasn't capable of miraculously saving everyone at the presidential rally. Asking one or two of these questions is like opening a theological Pandora's box: Suddenly, we are inundated with questions that should never see the light of day.

Questions like: If God is capable of saving someone from gun violence, then what is God doing when a shooter breaks into an elementary school? If God can perform lifesaving miracles, why is any child anywhere dying of disease? If God can change the outcome of political elections, why did he not prevent homicidal dictators from ever coming to power?

These questions don't feel good to ask. They are uncomfortable. To ask them is to lose our theological footing, to topple over, and to end up sprawled out in the darkness on the cold, cement basement floor. To avoid this discomfort, theology has developed strategies for responding to these questions as soon as they are uttered.

So, for example, some theologians might invoke a concept of free will, by which they might mean that God is mostly in control but that humans can decide to enact evil in the world. The question for them is whether God can ever override or manipulate human free will. If they believe that God can act to thwart the intentions of a would-be assassin, then the answer is yes. But then we might ask why God didn't prevent the assassination attempt any sooner than he did. Why wait until the very last minute? If God can intervene in humans affairs when the going gets tough, why not intervene before the going gets going?

Other theologians might be hesitant to say that God is capable of manipulating humans, but they might claim that he can step in to alter the laws of nature. Rather than, say, changing the heart of the attempted assassin, God merely intervened to cause the bullet to veer off its intended course. But if God can act in this way, then we might wonder why he didn't create a natural world in such a way that bullets couldn't travel through the air. If God is going to mess with the natural world, then why does it matter when he does it? Again, we are back to the same question: Why didn't God make it so that he didn't have to intervene in the first place?

I've called the above two responses "strategies," but they're really tricks. Sleights of hand. The magician-theologian who offers them is trying to distract us from looking at his right hand as it drops a coin in his pocket. "You were wanting to know why God allows bad things to happen, but look over here: free will. Ta da!" The point isn't to answer the questions but to dodge them, to redirect the questioner's attention to a point she isn't inclined to doubt.

To get out of tricky questions with linguistic sleights of hand—this is what "apologetics" has become. I first learned how to pull off these feats as an undergraduate student at Liberty University. The word "apologetics" comes from the Greek word for apology, which means defense. As Christians, we were taught, we should always be prepared, in the words of Paul, "to make your defense to anyone who demands from you an accounting for the hope that is in you" (1 Pet. 3:15). When I was a student, all freshmen were required to take two courses in apologetics, where we learned, basically, how to make atheist professors look unintelligent by asking two or three perfectly worded questions. For instance: "You say there are no absolute truths. Well, isn't that statement an absolute? Ta da!" The aesthetic of this sort of apologetics is what can only be called Nana-nana-boo-boo!

To take an example: If an "evolutionist" were to tell us that carbon dating proves the world is older than six thousand years, we would simply remind them that God creates things with signs of age. "That's why he created Adam as an adult and not a newborn." Another win for our team.

But what is the point of strategic theology? To be right? To get God right? Theology is a second-order reflection on a first-order experience. It is critical reflection on our intuitive awareness that we have been visited by God, that, as C. S. Lewis once put it, while we were playing cops and robbers in the basement, we heard an extra pair of footsteps in the darkness.[2]

The point of theology isn't to get God right, but to reflect on the fact that we've been got. Yes, right here, in the basement. We have a visitor.

The Trouble with All the Omnis

What kind of a God has gotten us?

Is it really the kind of God who saves one life by killing another? Who knows the gunman is coming, who can stop the gunman from coming, but who chooses not to for reasons having to do with . . . something about teaching us important lessons?

Some traditional conceptions of God describe him as being perfect in all his attributes, specifically perfect in knowledge, power, and goodness. This is the God best described by the prefix omni: omniscient, omnipotent, omnibenevolent. I have a hard time believing in this kind of God, mostly because I don't believe it's the God that the biblical and Christian traditions have consistently testified to. Even more, these characteristics don't sit comfortably next to each other, as Epicurus pointed out some three centuries before the birth of Jesus.

> Is God willing to prevent evil, but not able? Then he is not omnipotent. Is he able, but not willing? Then he is malevolent. Is he both

> able and willing? Then where does evil come from? Is he neither able nor willing? Then why call him God?[3]

Called the theodicy, this short argument points out the obvious: that the world has gone very wrong, and God either doesn't notice, doesn't care, or doesn't possess the ability to fix it. But if any of these are the case, "then why call him God?"

Responding to this challenge is an apologist's bread and butter. But let's not allow ourselves to be distracted by the red handkerchief in their left hand. Let's welcome the uncomfortable. Let's sit with it, become friends with it. As long as we're in the basement, we might as well ask questions that don't belong upstairs. Our asking, however, will not be the asking of apologetics. To explain or justify evil in light of God, or God in light of evil, does not interest me. In fact, it offends me. Not that we should steer clear of theology that offends: How else would feminist or queer or postcolonial theologies ever get done?! What I mean is, this kind of asking—asking for the purposes of being clever, for the purposes of "letting God off the hook," so to speak—offends my sense of justice. An entire town is destroyed by wildfire and we show up, apologetics in hand, to prove that God is X or Y even though Z just happened and ruined someone's life. The questions themselves aren't unjust, but our motivation (to respond to tragedy by offering simple answers) seems tone-deaf, unkind, and immoral. In the wake of tragedy, humans need space to ask uncomfortable questions, even ones that seem to impugn an all-knowing, all-powerful, all-loving God. If God is truly the third, then he should at the very least have enough patience for us as we muck around in the basement asking questions away from the ever-listening ears of the apologists.

Epicurus's questions take for granted that God has advanced knowledge of what might happen. We can't ask if God is willing and/or able to prevent evil if God doesn't know about the evil ahead of time. So we need to start with thinking about omniscience.

Omniscience, at least a certain notion of omniscience, is that divine attribute whereby God is magical enough to know all the bad stuff that will one day happen, but not magical enough to do anything about it. According to the doctrine of omniscience, God has perfect knowledge of all historical events, whether they happened, are happening, or will happen in the future. Thomas Aquinas, the thirteenth-century Dominican priest and theologian, wrote extensively about God's omniscience in the *Summa Theologicae*. The *Summa* is structured systematically, in a series of questions and answers, called a *disputatio*. In question 14 of the first part (*prima pars*), Thomas considers the "perfect knowledge" of God, according to which God "has knowledge even of things that are not." That's because, argues Thomas, "the present glance of God extends over all time, and to all things which exist in any time, as to objects present to Him."[4] God is, in other words, outside the timeline, so to speak, and has a bird's-eye view of history. All moments are to him *this* moment. All past and future are to him *present*.

Omniscience is one of those ideas that is entangled with so much of our theology. Getting rid of it will require us to rethink what we mean by "God" in the first place. For some of us, there is no "God" without omniscience. As I learned from my apologetics teachers, God is perfect in knowledge—if he isn't, then he's not God. A God who doesn't know the future is a contradiction in terms.

So, we might retort, is "knowing the future." It's perfectly acceptable to claim that God knows the past and the present, which is to say, God knows all that can be known. The future, by definition, cannot be known and so God doesn't know it. How could he? It hasn't yet happened. We can't simply make God the subject of nonsense sentences and then pretend that they now make sense.

Some defenders of omniscience take to sophisticated-sounding philosophy to make their case. It isn't that God knows future events, they reason, but the present truth value of all propositions. "Billy will choose to eat pepperoni pizza next Thursday." This statement is either true or false, goes the argument, and God knows which it is. God's knowledge of the future, then, isn't perceptive but propositional; he doesn't *see* what will happen, but he knows which sentence truthfully describes what will happen.

Like many an apologetic move, this one seems fishy. At first, we might feel that we've been had, but we soon come to realize that this sort of apologetics is just a little too philosophically tidy. Too systematic. Too sterile. If we're in the basement asking terrifying questions about God, the last thing we want is to be lectured about God's relationship to the present truth-claims of future states-of-affairs. Someone, we feel, is playing word games with us. Either God knows the future completely as it will be, or he doesn't.

My biggest problem with omniscience isn't that it seems to be a logical impossibility, but that it seems to be an *emotional* impossibility. At least for the kind of God that Christianity witnesses to, a loving God. Let's say you look out your window and see your child playing in the street, oblivious to the big truck hurling toward him. Based on the speed of the truck, you know its driver doesn't see your child. What do you do in this situation? You've told your kid not to play in the road, you've explained the risks and the consequences. Do you just let things play out to teach your child a lesson? Wouldn't knowing what will happen if you don't intervene compel you to intervene? Unless, of course, you didn't have the power to intervene.

This brings us to a discussion of the second omni —omnipotence, God's power. To what end does God know the future? To what use does he put that knowledge? I don't expect God to act on all his future knowledge, but surely knowing that some things will happen (like world war or mass genocide or plague) would cause him to act. I can't imagine any reason why God would know the Holocaust was going to happen but would sit back and watch it unfold. It's here our apologetic magician friend once again falls, pulls out his *free will* handkerchief, and starts waving it about wildly. *Look over here!* he tells us. *God can do everything he wants, but what he mostly wants is for us to make choices, good or bad.* This is sort of understandable to a point. However, our world is far past the point. I, for example, want my nephew to make good choices, which is why I encourage him to tell me which cereal he wants. But if he was about to make the choice to jump into the ocean without wearing a life vest,

I would very quickly override his free will. "Letting him choose to end his life" would not be the good I would want to secure in that scenario. Similarly, it's hard to imagine that a God who could intervene to prevent horrifying atrocities would simply choose not to, regardless of what lessons he had in mind.

It might feel uncomfortable, *basement-y* even, to play so cavalierly with ideas of omniscience and omnipotence. What kind of God are we left with if we purge him of these attributes? Well, first of all, we're left with a God who doesn't always see tragedy coming, even when it comes for him. (More on that later.) Secondly, we are left with a God who reflects more accurately the God who makes himself known in the narratives of scripture. As theologian Thomas Jay Oord writes, "Omnipotence is not born of Scripture."[5] In fact, he argues, "the Bible repeatedly describes creatures exerting power, often in opposition to what God wants."[6]

Oord points out another problem with omnipotence: It dies what philosophers call "the death of a thousand qualifications."[7] For instance, people who believe God can do everything don't actually believe that. They don't believe God can, say, will himself into nonexistence or fail to love us. They don't believe God can make a two-sided triangle. God cannot *not* be present somewhere in our world. These limitations fall under broader claims, such as "God cannot do what is illogical or ontologically contradictory" and God cannot undertake activities "that oppose God's nature."[8] Rather than spending so much time constructing the conditions under which God's omniscience and omnipotence "work," why not construct theologies that make better sense of the world that we are experiencing?

A world that goes wrong. A world whose every move does not seem planned. A world that seems to insist on calling its own shots.

What Does God Want?

In much Christian systematic theology, God's omnipotence is constrained by his omnibenevolence: He has the power to do everything he wants, and because he is all good, he doesn't will evil. But can we really be sure about what God wants?

Jesus sometimes argues for God's goodness based on how parents act toward their children. "Which one of you, if his son asks him for bread, will give him a stone? Or if he asks for a fish, will give him a serpent? If you then, who are evil, know how to give good gifts to your children, how much more will your Father who is in heaven give good things to those who ask him!" (Matt. 7:9–11, ESV). What Jesus is saying is that if we wouldn't act in ways that harm children, then why would God—who in Jesus's imagination is Father to all of us—act harmfully toward us?

But there are plenty of moments in scripture when God seems to act harmfully toward the creation he's supposed to love. I spent last year teaching freshmen how to work through the opening chapters of the book of Genesis. For many of them, it was their first time reading the stories—and they had strong feelings about them. The first two chapters are fine. God forms a good world from chaos and delights in its goodness. But when the serpent shows up, things go downhill pretty quickly.

Augustine taught the Western world how to read Genesis 3 (and because I was teaching at an Augustinian university, I taught students to read Augustine reading Genesis). God created Adam and Eve and planted them in the middle of a garden abounding with life and deliciousness. They only had one rule: Don't eat fruit from the tree in the middle of the garden. Well, the serpent convinced Eve to do so, and she convinced Adam to do so, and then God got angry at them, cursed them, and kicked them out of the garden. They thus became "sinful" and passed that defective, disobedient nature on to every other human. Although this is a popular Christian way of interpreting—a la Augustine, a la Paul—the garden story, there are other ways to read it. Many

Jews, for example, don't read it the way Augustine does. After all, if the story is about sin, then why doesn't that word ever show up in the text?[9] Perhaps the story isn't telling us about how humans messed up but about what humans are. But I digress.

Many of my students, without realizing how Augustine has worked on their theological imaginations, instinctively take God's side when reading the so-called Fall. The punishment was a little harsh, they reason, but Adam and Eve should have listened to God. But whom should God have listened to? To whom is he accountable? One student decided to go there. "I want to ask," he said, quietly but without hesitation, "if God knew what was going to happen, then why did he create the serpent in the first place?"

I didn't have an answer.

Most students don't ask those kinds of questions, at least on a Catholic campus. This particular student, though, was from Korea, which made me think he felt free to ask the question because he didn't have any cultural commitments to a text that is considered sacred by many of my students. Regardless, he was driving at something important. It seems as if God could have created a different kind of world, one without evil, or, if that weren't possible, at least one without snakes. Perhaps we can't blame God for the serpent—but can't we blame him for knowing what the serpent would do and creating him anyway? Or, to take the theological point outside of the Genesis story, even if God isn't responsible for the world's evil, he is still responsible for creating a world where evil was possible. I'm not sure that makes him look much better. True, our apologist friends promise us that *this* is the best possible world that God could have created given his desire of having humans freely love him. But surely a God of infinite creativity must have been able to come up with a better world. This world was the best idea? Really?

I'm not sure that it is. And God seems to have had shared this thought on more than one occasion. To take just one example:

> The LORD saw that the wickedness of man was great in the earth, and that every intention of the thoughts of his heart was only evil continually. And the LORD regretted that he had made man on the earth, and it grieved him to his heart. So the LORD said, "I will blot out man whom I have created from the face of the land, man and animals and creeping things and birds of the heavens, for I am sorry that I have made them. (Gen 6:5–7, ESV)

We're only six chapters into Genesis and God is already having second thoughts on making the kind of world that he did. In fact, he's asking himself the same questions that my student asked: Why *this* world? Can't God do better? God assumes he can, so he sends a flood to destroy all life: not just wicked humans, but their children and all the animals that live alongside them.

This, to me, seems like a very evil thing to do. Killing even one person just because you find their behavior to be at odds with your standards is immoral enough. But wiping out the entire human race, as well as most living animals, because you've judged their thoughts to be wicked? It's hard for me to square this with notions of God's omnibenevolence.

Perhaps, though, God agrees with me. Think of the rainbow from the story's resolution. Appearing more than seventy times in scripture, the word *qeset* primarily refers to the arched bow of a warrior.[10] God, as many Hebrew Bible passages point out, is a mighty warrior[11]; it makes sense that he is armed with a bow. When he's destroying the world with a flood, he's using his weapon, so to speak, to assault humanity. However, at some point, he relents and calls a truce. And to show he's serious, he turns his bow *on himself.* Luiz Gustavo Assis is one of several biblical scholars who point both to ancient literature and iconography to make the case that turning a bow away from your enemies and onto yourself was understood to signal a warrior's "non-hostile intent despite their capacity to harm."[12] It's as if after a shootout with you, I turn my gun on myself to remind you that I have a gun but that I'm not going to hurt you with it.

What is the story trying to tell us? Is God sorry for behaving so, well, monstrously? Does this mean he wishes he hadn't have killed everyone? This isn't a crazy suggestion. God has already admitted, earlier in the story, that he made a mistake. "The LORD saw that the wickedness of humankind was great in the earth, and that every inclination of the thoughts of their hearts was only evil continually. And the LORD *was sorry* that he had made humankind on the earth" (Gen. 6:5). Is the flood another of his mistakes?

This story seems to suggest that things don't always work out the way God counts on them to. What's more, he seems genuinely surprised by how the world ends up *worlding*. (I'm going to use this word a lot because it captures the dynamic quality of not only what the world is, but what it does: The world *worlds*.) The Noah story also shows that God sometimes regrets his own actions with the world. This regret implies that the world which has gone wrong *could have gone differently*. Does this mean God's plans don't always work out? Does it mean this current world, the post-flood world with all the rainbows, is really God's backup plan, his Plan B? But how many floods were there throughout our planet's history? Scientists tell us our world is living in the sixth extinction, a term Elizabeth Kolbert coined to describe the latest era on planet earth when a good deal of biodiversity goes extinct.[13] Does God regret all of these extinctions? Were they all his doing? If not, should God have intervened to prevent them from happening? Should he do so now that we are facing our own planetary demise? Or should God be getting ready to implement his seventh backup plan?

Once again, we're confronted with difficult questions: What kind of planner is a God who needs to execute backup plans? How all-knowing and all-powerful can he really be? And how *good*?

Does the Bible Tell Me So?

When we're talking about the story of Noah's flood, we're talking about myth. We are "going offline," so to speak, taking a break from the world of cold, hard facts and entering the world of story. We aren't trying to nail down who God is—as if we could do that!—we're trying to learn the best ways to talk about and think about his actions with the world, his history with us. Although we were not characters in the flood story, we nevertheless confess that we are members of a community that believes itself to be addressed by the God that Genesis is narratively constructing. Our goal is to interpret this and other stories within our believing communities so that we can address both God and the world with faith, confident that both God and the world are conversation partners,[14] even when and if the conversation runs dry.

Stories require interpretation. Stories don't simply speak; they are heard. But the quality of how we hear them depends on how we theorize our relationship to those stories. I hear scripture as one who believes himself to be addressed, called to account, summoned—not by scripture per se, but by the God under whose pressure the scriptures come to be. (Not *came* to be: the scriptures are dynamic and alive, and *come to be* whenever they are read, engaged, confessed, and yes, *questioned*.)

Scripture resists easy categorization. "The Bible" is a collection of different writings and oral traditions across a variety of genres spanning millennia that show us how our faith ancestors were responding to the God whom they believed had laid claim to them. Sometimes they get it wrong; sometimes we do; sometimes even God does. That's one lesson God learns from the flood: God rushed to judgment, and he shouldn't have. He should have questioned his interpretation of humanity as irredeemably evil. That's why God hangs his bow in the sky: not primarily as a sign to humans, but as a sign to himself, a sign to slow down, to reconsider his judgments, to question his own certainty of interpretation. "Take another look," the rainbow cautions God, "reconsider. There's more going on here than you think. Read it again."

But if Genesis shows us what happens when God rushes to judgment, it also shows us what happens when humans rush to judgment. Just a few verses after the Flood story concludes, the Bible narrates an incredibly bizarre episode:

> Noah, a man of the soil, was the first to plant a vineyard. He drank some of the wine and became drunk, and he lay uncovered in his tent. And Ham, the father of Canaan, saw the nakedness of his father, and told his two brothers outside. Then Shem and Japheth took a garment, laid it on both their shoulders, and walked backwards and covered the nakedness of their father; their faces were turned away, and they did not see their father's nakedness. When Noah awoke from his wine and knew what his youngest son had done to him, he said, 'Cursed be Canaan, lowest of slaves shall he be to his brothers.'" (Gen. 9:20–25)

Commentators have offered creative interpretations of this story, many of which I find fruitfully provocative. But if we boil the story down to its bare bones, we've got a male authority figure overreacting. Japheth sees his father naked—as many children probably do, by the way—and his father *curses* him eternally? It seems as if this brief narrative has been placed right after the flood story to remind readers of the dangers of rushing to judgment, a risk shared by both humans and their creator. Both we and God, these stories suggest, are emotional, sometimes fickle beings. We become angry, offended, irate, and if we're not careful, we make bad calls. Unplanned tragedy doesn't always just happen; it is sometimes our doing. That's why we need God; that's why he needs us.

Here I'm tempted to ask if the Bible "gets this one right." I don't mean this in a simplistic way, like "Did the flood really happen?" (probably not) or "What exactly did Japheth do to his father?" (why even go there?). What I mean is: Is the Bible's portrayal of God in the Flood story accurate? My apologist friends would be horrified to hear me ask this question. Of course, they would reply, "all Scripture is god-breathed" (2 Tim. 3:16, NIV). Well, so are humans but, according to the same scriptures, God didn't respect them enough to not drown them all, infants and toddlers included. If God can drown the God-breathed, then we can at least question it.

We need to be clear about what scripture is and what it isn't. In my opinion, the most helpful theorization of scripture comes from a Jewish theologian and bible scholar named Benjamin D. Sommer. In *Revelation and Authority*, Sommer outlines what he calls a participatory theology of revelation, which understands revelation as involving "active contributions by both God and Israel."[15] Sommer suggests we see the Bible not itself as "a revelation" from God, but as "a response to God's act of revelation."[16] Rather than interpreting the revelation of God at Sinai in a sense where God literally writes the law and offers it to Israel, Sommer argues that revelation is the awareness of "a sense of commandedness, which yielded paraphrasing in the form of law."[17] This sense of commandedness precedes us, rushes in upon us, grasps us, and once we realize that we are grasped, it is our turn to respond. The freedom we have in formulating our response(s) to God's revelation does not overshadow or minimize God's action. As Sommer says, "Israel completes the sentence that begins 'God commands us to,' but God remains the subject, and the verb does not lose its basic meaning of requiring obedience."[18] God's revelation must be responded to so that it can become what it is. God speaks through those who hear God speak. Or, to put it differently, the interpretation of revelation is an integral part of what we mean by revelation.

This isn't to reduce revelation to something *merely* subjective. In fact, Sommer's definition helps us maintain the gap between the revealer and those interpreting what the revealer is revealing. Not that this line is hard and fast and clearly demarcated. Revelation requires work, both on God's part and ours. God reveals God to us, and then we try, as a community, to make sense of his visitation. Sometimes we arrive at a consensus—the Bible is one such consensus—but even when we land on some meaning, we're not off the hook. We have to keep listening for God's revelation, which means we have to keep speaking it. And to speak is to interpret.

With this definition of "revelation," we can go back to the story of Noah's flood and engage with it in new ways. No longer do we need to waste our time wondering if the flood really happened the exact way it's narrated; instead, we can focus on how God's character is coming-to-be in this particular text. The main action of God destroying creation is beyond the pale; there's no way for us to make excuses for his actions. What's done is done. There's no taking it back. But if we take a more capacious look at how God's character is coming-to-be, and coming to be understood, in the opening chapters of Genesis, then we can piece together a few important things.

First, what the story of the flood shows us is that God is really affected by what goes on in the world. He responds with fits of rage, with jealousy, with frustration. He has a complicated personality because—and this is the point the Bible wants to make sure we keep front and center—God is a person. We'll unpack this a little more as we go on, but what's important to remember is that at the center of the universe is not some unmoved mover but a person who longs to be in relationship with the world he's created.

To be fair, if what God wanted was relationship with his world, then his murderous rampage was self-defeating. But—and this is the second takeaway—at the time of the flood, God was still figuring out the best way to be not just God, but *this* God. God is always becoming God in new ways. As a Christian, I believe Jesus is the prime example of this new and creative coming-to-be. But the process of God-becoming-God predates Jesus. As long as God *gods* on behalf of a world, he is constantly coming-to-be in new ways in response to that world. God, at least this God, *is*, we might say, his response to a world; he comes to be as he responds to the world; his response reveals his identity because his response constitutes his identity.

Third, the Noah story tells us that God doesn't know in advance or control everything that goes on in this world. If he could, then why would he have been caught off guard by humans' wicked behavior? That seems to suggest he isn't omniscient; and the fact that he doesn't just wave a magic wand and make humans behave the way he wants them to suggests certain inabilities on his part. God does use (and misuse!) power in this story; but it's a Plan B kind of power, the kind of power he didn't want to have to use, an after-the-fact kind of power which you put into play after things don't go the way you hoped. Love: This is the power to start over, to begin again, to make all things new. It is, as we will see, the power of love.

But the problem with God's initial response to human wickedness, his Plan B, is that God didn't want to make all things new . . . he wanted new things. That's very different. The second one means throwing up your hands, throwing out the art project, pulling out a new canvas, and starting from scratch. The first, in contrast, means taking what's already there and refashioning it, transforming it. Not throwing it out but taking it up, taking it to yourself, and reminding it, "Look, we're going to figure it out together. You are going to be beautiful. *You are going* to be beautiful!" It's this response—Plan C, let's call it—that God ultimately settles on.

I don't like the story of Noah's flood, but I think when we keep an eye out for liberation and life, then we can read the text reparatively.[19] Our ancestors in faith found themselves to be wrapped up in a can't-ever-quit-you relationship with God, and they tried to "get at" that relationship with stories and poetry and words. Some of those words, I believe, get it wrong—I don't believe God wiped out an earth full of babies and toddlers just because he thought their parents were sinful. And in fact, it's because I affirm the overwhelming testimony of scripture—that God is madly in love with his world—that I don't believe God is emotionally capable of doing what Genesis 6 says he did. But I nevertheless believe that there is something sacred going on in these texts, which narrate a group of humans responding to the event of God's revelation, working their hardest to interpret it. They might have gotten the details wrong, but they got something important right, and it's this that will help us as we try and make sense of God's relationship to a world gone wrong.

Rather than show us that God has a plan for the world, the early flood story tells us that the creator God has *hope* for the world, hope that it will turn out well, that it will become the best version of itself, that it will eventually become the world he dreamed of when he said, "Let there be." God's hopes are frustrated, but he can't just wipe his hands of the world and start over—that's why he places his bow in the sky. God sees that the world has become very wrong, but he has determined to not start over from scratch. He has made a pact with the world. Whatever he is going to do, he is going to do with *this* world. You don't throw away a world gone wrong. You make it right. And that is just what he hopes to do.

The question is, will God get what he hopes for?

Beyond Slogans

While I was working on this chapter, giant fires raged in Los Angeles. In all, more than sixteen thousand structures and thirty-seven thousand acres have been destroyed. The fires have been devastating, displacing many people, and bankrupting countless others. Lives have been ruined, families torn apart, dreams shattered. As humans are wont to do when tragedy strikes, many of us search for God, hoping for him to show up.

For some people, though, God has already shown up. That's why the fires happened, at least according to the social media theologians (of whose number there is no end). One post, clearly photoshopped, depicts a home with a bright red roof standing completely untouched in the middle of a neighborhood filled with charred rubble. The home was said to have belonged to a Christian, which is why God preserved it. The photo is captioned with a passage from Psalm 91 (NIV): "No harm will overtake you, no disaster will come near your tent; For he will command his angels concerning you to guard you in all your ways." The gist is clear: God saved the Christian's home from fire, but didn't intervene on behalf of any of the godless around him.

Let's imagine, for the moment, the photo presents a real image. How do we know, first of all, that no other Christians live in the burned-down neighborhood? Are there really no Christians—or Jews; let's remember the Psalms belong first to Jews—in any of the neighborhoods that burned down? None?! Let's take it further. In another horrifying story from Genesis, God promises to save an entire city for the sake of just ten righteous people who lived there. Why wouldn't the same logic apply in LA? If it is the case that just a handful of righteous people live in LA—and according to the meme, they do—then why doesn't God spare the city on their behalf? Better yet, why doesn't he spare the city *on his own behalf*? He's the one who loves his creation. It's not only homes that were destroyed; plenty of animals and trees and flowers were ruined too. Why is he killing the land because he's angry with humans? We also have to wonder what the point of the fires is. If God really wants to convince humans to repent, then why doesn't he just, you know, change their hearts? If he's powerful enough to send wildfires and control their progression, why can't he simply force, or better yet, *persuade* the atheist Hollywood execs to become born again?

Social media has done a number on humans, but some of its most pernicious effects have been theological. Rather than grapple with meaning, the way that Jacob wrestled with an angel,[20] we now do theology via meme. To wit: God saved a Christian's home from wildfire. Or: God saved President Trump from assassination. Or: This hurricane is part of God's plan.

To be fair, Christians have been at this game for a long time. When I was growing up in the nineties, we believed sharing the gospel was as simple as wearing special flip-flops on the beach: "Jesus Saves," we'd imprint in the sand, as we walked self-righteously by sinners showing too much skin. Jesus saves from what? From whom? Saves to what end? For what purpose? None of those questions mattered. The important bits were in the sand. Like an Ikea bookshelf, you can piece together the Gospel simply from looking at the barebones messaging it's been packed with.

Sure, some very important theological truths are simple and can be stated forthrightly. In some ways, this is what early creeds do: distill complicated doctrines down to pithy, easily memorized and confessed statements. But these credal statements were never intended to end theological conversation but to get it going, to help it along, to steer it down the right corridors. To open the confessors up to mystery, not to close us off to further questioning, and certainly not to keep us away from the basement. In fact, according to our creeds, Jesus, our Lord, suffered, died, and descended into hell. Talk about the basement! These might be shorthands, but they are anything but simple-minded memes.

I have to admit: I understand the impulse to find quick answers. When wildfires break out, it's somewhat comforting to believe that God is still in control of everything. When our loved ones suddenly die, it's helpful to remember that God predestined the time and place of their death. When the doctors find a lump, it can help to remember that this is all somehow part of God's plan. I used to believe all of this because it felt better than believing the alternative: that God wasn't in control, that God didn't know it was going to happen, that God didn't have a plan, and that even if he did, this fire, this death, this cancer wasn't it.

But now that I've spent some time in the basement, I've realized that pinning tragedy on some divine, inscrutable will isn't the balm I used to think it is. A god who stands idly by as the world goes wrong in exactly the way he knew it would . . . that's not the god for me. Nor is it the god for the communities that left us Genesis: The rainbow is a testimony *against* blaming disaster on God; it's his promise that he's gotten out of the Punishment Via Natural Disaster business. Nor is it the god of scripture who, time and time again, seems surprised, taken off guard, shocked at what has happened to his creation, and unable to get things immediately back on track, at least not on his own.

It's scary to write sentences like that. They go against all my apologetic instincts, instincts that I've long ago unlearned but that nevertheless, like much popular evangelical theology, still retain a chokehold on me. But Christian theology must begin with the Word made flesh—and the flesh of this world is rotting and oozing and falling off the bone. This world, the one that wounds us, that betrays us, the one which we will one day leave and which in the meantime mocks all our attempts at staying safe and healthy, this is the world in which we do theology. This is the world in which God reveals himself to us, in which we work out our response to this revelation, in which we come to hear and to say—with both reverence and scorn, terror and wonder, hope and disappointment—the name of God.

TWO

God of the Orphans and Widows

How God becomes God

"Father of orphans and protector of widows
is God in his holy habitation."

—PSALM 68:5

"You're on the verge of saying something you don't say."

I was halfway finished writing my dissertation. John Caputo ("Jack" to his friends), a member of my committee, was pushing me to fall one way or the other. I'd just shared a reading of Psalm 82, where God becomes God and then is invited to become God once again, or, depending on how you interpret it, invited to become even more God. The challenge put to me was whether God "is" beyond our theologizing about God. Or, as Jack phrased it: "Does God empty without remainder into our God-talk?" In other words, is my God-talk all there is to God? Is there any "God" beyond my theology? I imagine there might be, and yet I have no way of getting beyond my God-talk. So if there is any God that does not empty out into my God-talk, then I have no way of accessing him. And yet I still hope there is something there. Well, no, not something—because God is not some-*thing*. And certainly not *there*—because where would a not-being-talked-about God be located? Heaven? But now we're back to *our* God-talk. I hate when Jack asks me questions like this. Because he forces me to realize that I am indeed on a verge.

To be located on a verge is to encounter and play with ambiguity. The verge is that threshold from which we emerge, the moment preceding our emergence. The verge is a spatiotemporal metaphor for that which makes possible our ability to think and act, the time before time that makes possible the time of our decision. The verge is a place of indecision, but it's also a place of faith. It's a place where the knowledge of what is begins to give way to the hope of what might be.

Our God-talk is *about* God—what is it, *who* is it, that we are talking about? Does he have any existence beyond our talking about him? Our talking with and to him? Do our prayers and liturgies contribute anything to God? Does God come to be in a new way when God is praised and petitioned? When God is responded to?

There is something *verginal* about the name of God. In a creative reading of God's revelation to Moses in a burning bush on Mount Horeb, Richard Kearney notes that God's revelation of his name depends in no small part on Moses's response. Here's the Exodus passage.

> And the angel of the Lord appeared to him in a flame of fire out of the midst of a bush. He looked, and behold, the bush was burning, yet it was not consumed. And Moses said, "I will turn aside to see this great sight, why the bush is not burned." When the Lord saw that he turned aside to see, God called to him out of the bush, "Moses, Moses!" And he said, "Here I am." Then he said, "Do not come near; take your sandals off your feet, for the place on which you are standing is holy ground." (Exodus 3:2–5, ESV)

But where is the "here" where Moses and God meet? They are occupying a place together, but a distance, a gap remains between them. This is not a physical boundary, like the distance between two poles, but the verge that yawns between a call and its response. God has heard the cries of his people and has visited Moses to urge him to act on his behalf. But why doesn't God act on his own behalf? Why go through a middleman? Surely God can do it best alone! But the story doesn't lead to that conclusion. If God is to act, then Moses is going to need to act. A Moses-less action of God doesn't seem possible, at least according to the theological imagination of the Exodus story.

When God first reveals himself to Moses, he says that he is "the God of your father, the God of Abraham, the God of Isaac, and the God of Jacob." He does not reveal himself as being, but as *being-for* or *being-with*. He does not reveal himself to be God, but to be a God-*of*. The people on whose behalf he gods seem to constitute his *to-be*. Moses wanted God's name; the only names he got were the names of his ancestors. That's because the name of God is unnameable apart from those whose names he keeps. God is "of" Abraham, Isaac, and Jacob the way that a molecule is "of" hydrogen and oxygen. God is forever entangled with these three people. As far as God is concerned, he has no identity without his people.

When we read the story in this way, a few theological implications emerge. First, the Exodus narrative, as well as biblical narrative on the whole, is not concerned properly with God, but with *this* God. Who God might have been before he became *this* God is not important to the Bible. And so, I suppose, it isn't that important to me. Christian theology does not reflect on and engage with the god of the philosophers, but of Abraham, Isaac, and Jacob, of Moses and Miriam, of you and me. Christian theology is concerned with a god who loves, a god whose godness consists precisely in his loving.

Second, who God *is* is what he does: He is a God who moves out of himself to be with that which is not God. This is a god of "function rather than substance," says Kearney, "relation rather than abstraction."[1] If we, like Moses, take our theological cue while gazing at a burning bush, then we realize that our divine visitor is "a god who does rather than a being who is."[2] God's identity, his *this*-ness, depends on what he does for the world that he has created.

Third, that God names himself in this way seems to imply that his identity remains at least partially open. If God is of and with and for his people, then who he is remains bound up with what and whom his people choose to become. God—as in, the God that God becomes, the God who Paul hopes will one day be "all in all" (1 Cor. 15:28)—is "the name of a promise"[3], the promise that God might become God.

Will he make good on this promise? Will *we*? If God's being is being-for, then God's being depends on that which he is *for*, which is terrifying because, well, that's us. And we haven't exactly been on our best behavior. Our world is full of violence and exploitation and hate. If we survive the climate change fiasco (and there aren't any guarantees we will), we will quite likely continue to squander away our time in front of screens, and offload as much of our humanity as we can onto AI. If God becomes alongside the world that constitutes his *of*, then what kind of God is he becoming?

And if we're going to say that God *might* become the God he hopes to become, then—remember, we're in the basement—we have to admit that things might work out otherwise. What if our world ends in nuclear holocaust? What if there are no descendants of Abraham, Isaac, and Jacob left for him to look after? What is a god without a people to god for?

These ideas might seem like nothing more than the theological intrigues of a contemporary academic, but in fact they appear in some of our oldest biblical texts. "Will God become all that God might become?" is not primarily a contemporary theological reflection but an ancient biblical taunt. And it's hurled right at God.

Psalm 82

The psalm I was puzzling over at the beginning of this chapter is my favorite passage in the entire Bible: Psalm 82, which John Dominic Crossan has called "the single most important text in the Christian

Bible."[4] I agree. Every story, every parable, every credal formula written in the New Testament takes for granted the theology that the singers of Psalm 82 were creatively groping after. In this chapter, I want to spend some time thinking, or better yet, *poeticizing* with the theopoetics of Psalm 82, and then extend that poeticizing beyond the text in the attempt of speaking "God" responsibly in a world gone wrong. Let's begin with the psalm itself.

A PSALM OF ASAPH

God takes the stand in the Divine Council,
In the midst of all the gods he issues judgment.

"How long will you judge unjustly,
And show favor to the wicked?

Make justice for the vulnerable and fatherless,
Vindicate the needy and impoverished,

Deliver the vulnerable and the wretched,
Snatch them away from the hand of the wicked.

They don't know — neither will they understand.
They walk about in darkness.
All the earth's foundations are shaking loose.

For a while, I convinced myself that you were gods,
Sons of the Most High, all of you.

But in fact, you shall die like the no-gods you are,
Fall as even the mightiest humans do."

Arise, O God, judge the earth justly,
For all the nations you're inheriting are now
counting on you.[5]

To begin to make sense of this psalm, we have to understand it within the mythology of the ancient Near East. Although plenty of commentators have translated this song to narrate a contentious meeting between God and human rulers, many scholars believe it's best understood as a meeting of the divine council, a staple of Near Eastern mythology. According to Janus Lemański, the divine council "is derived from the Canaanite tradition of the hierarchy in the world of deities."[6] One god takes his stand in the assembly and brings an accusation against other deities. And what is it that the gods of Psalm 82 are being accused of? Simply put: They aren't *godding* the way a true god is supposed to.

Erich Zenger says the psalm "presupposes the ancient Near Eastern notion that the world is based on a divine order of law that is meant to be defended and carried out by the gods within the territories assigned to them."[7] These gods are judging dishonestly, favoring the wicked, not rescuing those who need their help. The gods are failing those in their charge and now the entire world—the very material structure of the universe itself—is at risk of falling apart at the seams. "All the earth's foundations are shaking loose!" says the psalm.

And so, God must act. If the world is to be saved, God must rise up and pronounce the death of the gods. They are failing to uphold their duties, failing to take responsibility for those in their charge. They are behaving like non-gods, and God—the God who becomes The One God—will not tolerate that.

Over and over in scripture, God expresses concern for "widows and orphans." For instance, in Exodus 22:22 (ESV), God commands his people to "not mistreat any widow or fatherless child," threatening that those who ignore his command will see his wrath. And in Deuteronomy 10:17–18, Israel's God—"the God of gods and Lord of lords"—is said to "execute justice for the fatherless and widow." Concern for widows and orphans is a bedrock principle of Israel's conception of God.

The phrase "orphans and widows" is a biblical metonymy, which occurs when one group of people stands in for a larger group of people. Just as

"Hollywood" refers to those who work in the film industry, "orphans and widows" is a catch-all term for all those who are victims of misfortune. Psalm 82 wants to drive the point home, however, so it reworks the traditional vocabulary, breaking up the word pairs into new combinations. Rather than being concerned for the orphans and widows, the god of Psalm 82 is concerned for "the vulnerable and the fatherless" and "the needy and impoverished." Perhaps this word change reflects an ethical development, as Zenger suggests.[8] God cares about all the unlucky—which is most of us, at one time or another. A real God doesn't lose sight of anyone. The gods that The One God takes to task have done just that: They have overlooked the overlookable, which is, within the mythology of Psalm 82, a capital offense. So God acts.

Verse six is notoriously difficult to translate. The King James Version renders it "I have said, ye are gods," perhaps to bring out the fact that the speaker *used to think* these beings were divine. The main idea here is that God was under the impression that the others in the Divine Council were, like him, gods. But this assessment was wrong. To bring this out, I translate the verse like this: "For a while, I convinced myself that you were gods" (v. 6). To appreciate the sassiness of this verse, I encourage my students to hear it the way a drag queen might say it: "I had thought that y'all was gods, but then I SAW the way you were ACTING. Thank you, NEXT!" The God of Israel might have originally assumed his colleagues were gods just as he was; however, their behavior has convinced him he was wrong. "Because they do not match the concept of God proclaimed by this psalm," says Zenger, the God of Israel strips them of their "claims to power," rendering them "functionless."[9] With nothing to do, they have *no one to be*. And so, indeed they "shall die like the no-gods" they are (v. 7).

A god usurping others deities' power is nothing unique to the mythology of Psalm 82. What is unique, however, is the method of usurpation. Unlike Baal who destroys Yam, or Marduk who disembowels Tiamat, God wins this battle with his words. Sure, he has pronounced death on the vanquished deities, but this isn't anything violent—only gods live forever; the Artists Formerly Known as Gods will therefore die, like the no-gods they are. Not only do we learn from this psalm that God's character is compassionate and just, we also learn that he can respond to, and defeat, hate and injustice with nonviolence. Those qualities will not live into God's future; they have an expiration date.

If the first seven verses of Psalm 82 tell a story of deicide, the final verse shifts into liturgy: "Arise, O

God, judge the earth justly, for all the nations you're inheriting are now counting on you." He has spent the psalm taking other gods to task for their failures. It's now time for him to show them how it's done, for him to actualize the deity that he himself has been defining. With the other deities no longer acting as patrons to the nations, God himself now takes possession of their spoils. It's time for him to arise on behalf of the entire world.

One often overlooked takeaway of the psalm is that while God emerges as The One God, things could have gone differently. In fact, they still might. If God's status as One God was an accomplishment, then that means it's not guaranteed. There was always a risk he wouldn't beat out the other gods in the divine council. Does that risk still exist today? He overcame injustice and apathy at some point in the past; but injustice and apathy seem to be still with us. Are they an ongoing threat to God's divinity? He has taken his stand with the poor and the lowly, thrown in his cards with the wretched. We know all too well what will happen to the marginalized if oppression continues to stamp them out. Do we know what will happen to their God? What is a god without a people to god for? Without people to shout to him "Arise"? Without people to urge him to become the God that other gods could not become?

God has spent the majority of Psalm 82 outlining the deities' failures. It's now his turn to do what they couldn't. They didn't help the poor and needy; will he? They didn't practice justice; will he? When a congregation sang, "Arise, O God, judge the earth justly," they weren't simply making nice music. There were real stakes, cosmic stakes, involved. Shouting "arise," says Zenger, "urges YHWH to bring to realization . . . the divinity that he himself has defined . . . for the rescue of the chaos-threatened cosmos."[10] God seems to have very specific ideas of what divinity ought to be, but now those ideas need to be enacted. God has landed the role; he must now perform. "Arise!"

But why tell God to "Arise?" Why not conclude the psalm with thanking him for eradicating injustice once and for all, for defining and enacting divinity, and for rescuing the universe from annihilation? Why implore him to god the way a real god ought to? He's just going to do it, anyway, right?

Right?

And you thought we were no longer in the basement.

How Long, O Lord?

The prayer for God to arise begins with an acknowledgment of failure: that God has not yet totally arisen. The prayer for God to arise is a prayer for God to become all he believes a god should be. Why pray for him to arise if he's already done it, if he's already become all that he might become?

Admitting God's failure to act on his people's behalf might seem audacious, but the writers of scripture aren't embarrassed by their audacity. The psalms show this poignantly.

> How long, O LORD? Will you forget me for ever?
> How long will you hide your face from me?
> How long must I take counsel in my soul,
> and have sorrow in my heart all day long?
> (Ps. 13:1–2a, ESV)

In *Creation and the Persistence of Evil,* Jon D. Levenson notes how some biblical passages invoke God's defeat of chaos only to contrast his former victory with his current losing streak. In these texts, Levenson argues, "The contradiction between the God of the myth and the God of current historical experience has risen to the level of consciousness."[11] God's power is recalled for the express purpose of cutting him down to size. This is how I hear the closing refrain of Psalm 82. "Arise!" is not only an invocation—it's a taunt. *Arise like we know you can! What are you waiting for?*

Both questions—when will God arise? What is he waiting for?—go largely unanswered in scripture. The closest we get to answers are vague adumbrations about God's future, discussed poetically in terms like "kingdom of God," "Day of the Lord," and so forth. God is acting now, and God will act even more decisively any day now, sometime very soon, perhaps before we finish this sentence. This, however, provides little comfort. We are still left looking to the skies and urging God to arise, wondering why he won't, wondering whether he truly can.

There is another question, however, the Bible is clearer about it, and that concerns God's preferred method of activity. *How* will God act? Recall what Kearney said about God's revelation: The call of God requires the response of Moses. God's identity is bound up with Moses's "Here I am." Levenson makes a similar point. "God depends, as it were, upon the witness of Israel: without it, his divinity is not realized. The actualization of the full potential of God requires the testimony of his special people."[12] This is why Kearney translates the name of God revealed in Exodus 3 as "I am who may be if you continue to keep my word and struggle for the coming of justice."[13] Perhaps there are other kinds of gods in other kinds of worlds whose happening has nothing to do with how those in their charge respond to their happening. It's just that the God we meet in the Bible only happens when humans help him happen, only arises when humans tell him to arise.

What happens, though, in the interim between our praying for God to arise and God's arising? It seems that this space, however we define it, is where we are currently located. It is a space where hope and anxiety merge: the hope that God will soon arise and the anxiety that bubbles up when we are forced to admit he has not yet risen. This space is a place of might. Hope and foreknowledge are not synonymous. We hope that God will arise; he might not. But he might! And the might of God is mighty indeed: God is in fact the mightiest—not in the sense of valor but of possibility.

I have to admit: The order of Psalm 82 makes me a little uneasy. The God who becomes the One God arises in victory, and then the psalm singers ask him to arise. The obvious implication is that he has not yet overthrown the powers of injustice the way he promised he would. But if that's the case, then it seems that God has failed in the same way the other gods have failed: None of them seem to be doing anything about injustice and hatred and apathy. The God of Psalm 82 vanquishes the other gods precisely because they are not all that they could be. They have not lived up to their potential. But neither has the God who replaced them, which is why we must sing him this psalm in the first place. Should we, instead, pray for a new God to show up and overthrow the One God because he's not *godding* the way a God should?

By the time the psalm singers pray for God to arise, urgent theological questions have emerged, questions about the relationship between God's action and our prayers for him to arise, about God's character, God's *abilities*. Perhaps the psalm is suggesting that if justice and concern for the needy do not win the day, then God will cease to become God, at least *this God*, the one who is moved by the world's suffering. God has no being apart from God's concern for the wretched of the earth. The moment God stops having this concern, he stops being God. An unconcerned God is no god at all.

From god to God

The psalms aren't systematic theology; they are prayers, and they flow from the lives of those who prayed them. They do not sound like the typical prayers we say at church. These are prayers that cut God down to size, prayers that hope for the brutal slaughter of enemies, prayers that give expression to the thoughts we try to keep away from polite company. They are, in short, prayers we feel comfortable uttering alone in the basement.

Compared with many of its peers, Psalm 82 is not that bleak, at least not on the surface. No babies' heads are dashed against rocks, none of God's enemies are consumed by fire. God does not wage violent war with the pantheon; he simply out-gods them and they vanish away. Still, the psalm is troubling. Because it doesn't end on a high note ("Arise!") but with a crunchy, dissonant suspension ("Arise . . ."). The needy are still in need; orphans and widows are still neglected; injustice is wreaking havoc on the created order. And God is . . . where? In a far-off council room making a case before El? Standing at the ready to arise on behalf of the impoverished? But not with them and arising for them?

The question "Where is God?" is a different version of the question "Why is God not currently acting?" It's a question not of location but of activity. The psalm singers are convinced that God has compassion for them, but they are equally convinced that their world does not always give evidence to this compassion. God is love; the world has gone wrong. How do we reconcile these statements? Some theologians retreat into diagrams and scholastic proofs for the existence of God. I prefer to crawl inside the mythical world of Psalm 82 and pray. (There is in fact no better way to "do theology.")

To be sure, we can't pretend that Psalm 82 says all there is to say about God. Some of the ideas in the psalm are in need of refinement, even correction—in fact, we might see other psalms that presuppose monotheism to be such a corrective. But I think it marks an important point in the development of what we now call "biblical theology." Zenger says that Psalm 82 could be described "as a poem about the transition from mythology to a monotheistic frame of reference."[14] If the poem begins in a pantheon, it ends in God's throne room. The psalm offers two competing views of god—and then plants its flag firmly in one of those camps. The poem thus, in the words of Bible scholar Matitiahu Tsevat, "represents a watershed in the history of ideas" by setting open "the course for future religious development."[15]

In other words, the text of Psalm 82 contains traces of the theological journey that the people eventually called Israel underwent as they wrestled with their ideas about God and God's relationship with their gone-very-wrong world. What is fascinating about this journey is that it shows the development of Jewish monotheism to be inseparably bound up with the development of ethics. God achieves his being by performing in certain ways. God is not compassionate simply because he is the only god there is; he is the only God there is because he is compassionate. The psalm, then, does not ground God's character in his existence. God's existence emerges from his new performances of divinity. God becomes God only as he loves. He loves himself into being (to echo the provocative claim of Jean-Luc Marion[16]).

Psalm 82 is a literary-ethical performance that shows us how ancient Israel was working out the event that happens in the name of God. The psalm shows that the creators and singers were very interested in questions of justice and compassion and solidarity, because, they learned, God was too. They certainly felt themselves to be summoned by a god who has his eyes on the lowly of the earth. This god has rushed in on the psalm singers, laid claim to them. This rushing in is what we mean by revelation. The psalm singers had a revelation of God, and they tried to work out that revelation in terms that made sense to them. Although the ancient trope of a battling divine council is deployed, the theology that started to emerge was poetically exploring a new concept of god. In this poem, God's coming to be is not ontological, but ethical: Psalm 82 shows how God comes to be in a certain way, how God comes to be *this* God. As he manifests his compassionate character, he asserts his authority over those deities for whom love is not an integral aspect of their divinity.

Granted, God comes to be in other ways in other texts. The Hebrew Bible does not provide a uniform account of God's relationship with the created world. In Job, for example, God has absolute sovereignty over his creation; it is only because God stands beyond the world's capricious worlding that Job feels that he can put his trust in him. I do not pretend, then, that the concept of God I am offering here is representative of mainstream biblical theology. All I'm doing is trying to reimagine the God/world relationship along trajectories that have been opened up by Psalm 82. And in this text, God becomes God because he out-loves everyone else. God's character is not a result of *but a grounding for* his being. He exists because he loves, and what he loves affects who he is. God is entangled with the world he has created. God is becoming God alongside the world in its becoming. Who God might become next depends in no small part on what the world accidentally evolves into.

This leads us to an inescapable question: Will God suffer the same fate as our world? But if that is so, then what anchors our hope? What, in fact, are we hoping for? We will have to come back to these questions at the end of our enquiry.

Arise!

I don't love being down here in the basement. The longer I stare through the darkness at various bric-a-brac, the more clearly it morphs into the startling figures of nightmares. A god whose identity is bound up forever with the world that he loves? A god who seems to need us to become all that he wishes to become? A god who is concerned for the orphans and widows, but hasn't yet taken definitive action to alleviate their suffering? This is frightening theology.

I wish I could believe in a different God. I wish I could believe in a god who solves all our problems, who has the power to do anything he wants to, who can override the natural processes of our world to overthrow the unjust and to rescue the needy. But on behalf of the orphans and widows, on behalf of the afflicted and downtrodden, on behalf of the marginalized, the oppressed, the wounded; on behalf of my friend whose husband suddenly dropped dead of a heart attack, on behalf of my friend who lost the twins she was carrying; on behalf of these and all the other hurting people in the world, who look to the heavens and wonder why God hasn't arisen; on behalf of the world itself whose climate is heating, whose sea levels are rising, whose animal populations are diminishing; for their sakes, I refuse to put my trust in an all-powerful god who can predict the future like a fortune teller and troubleshoot problems like a technician at a call center. To believe in an omniscient, omnipotent God is to betray the world which believes itself to be betrayed by its God.

And yet, from within the silent darkness of the basement, a silence that is pierced only by an occasional drip from a pipe sticking out of a wall, something within me whispers the word "Arise."

The very moment I am tempted to write off God as nothing but a projection of human ambition, I find this word welling up from a deep corner inside of me. "Arise!" It's a word of hope, a word that sounds forth because it remains convinced that God will in fact make good on our prayer for him to arise. But where does it come from? This situation of hopelessness can't have produced it. Why would I hope that our world would turn out better if this world is all that it's supposed to be?

This isn't "proof" that God exists—and anyway, theopoetics doesn't worry about proofs. But it is, well, notable. Our world is very wrong, yet we are very *hopeful*. Why? Why do we call on God to arise? Why do we trust that he will? Why do we believe that when he arises, the world will be put right? Here, the words of C. S. Lewis come to mind: "If we find in ourselves a desire that nothing in this world can satisfy, the most probable explanation is that we were made for another world."[17] Well, I don't quite go all the way with this sentiment: My desires are not for a different world but for *this world* to be different. Nonetheless, Lewis has got his finger on something.

Are we really to believe that our hopes and desires grow organically from a world that can neither sustain nor fulfill them?

If I, like the psalm singers, call on God to arise, it's only because God has first given me this word. My call for God to arise is not properly a call, but a response—a response to a God who, first of all, shows up. A God who is always already *of* us and with us and for us. I call on God to arise because he provokes me to. God *is* the provocation that stirs me not to throw my head back in resignation but to lift it to the skies and to scream for God to become what and who he promises to become.

This call, this provocation, is not another name for something reducible to this world. God might need Moses to help him along, but there is still a gap between them. "Take off your shoes, and come only this far," God tells him. How can we mark the space between Moses and God, or, more generally, between God and world? Where do we locate this verge, the one Jack finds me fidgeting on top of? We don't. It's there, but we can't point to it. It's the distance between Moses and God as they begin to journey toward each other. Not the distance between two localizable places, but the distance between a call and a response. God's relation to Abraham, Isaac, and Jacob, God's relation to the world he so loves, is a relation *of*. The boundary isn't between the physical world and a nonphysical world, but between a world that discovers itself being loved and the lover who is loving it, between a world desperate for God to arise and a God who is provoking it to hopefully call on him to arise.

Make no mistake: This provoking force is not a thing, but a person. This is what the Bible means by ascribing personhood to God. As Wolfhart Pannenberg pointed out, to say that God is a person is to say that God is nonmanipulable. "Whatever permits of being manipulated—if not at the moment, then still in principle—becomes a thing. Only that is a person which has a hidden, inner side and is not completely transparent to thought, so that it confronts one as an independent being."[18] Because God chooses to act unpredictably (that is, he is not bound to respond to the world on the world's own terms), God is a person; "events occur at his initiative in unforeseeable ways."[19] Hope does not naturally follow from this dreary sequence of events we call history. Hope is not a spontaneous occurrence that bubbles up organically from the depths of hopelessness. Hope must be unnaturally provoked within us, and provoked by a person who hopes he can make good on our hope.

The hope that God provokes within me is like a consuming fire shut up in my bones, keeping my soul warm and flickering in this cold, dark basement of a world.

The Theopoetics of Hope

I like thinking of God within the imaginaries constructed by Psalm 82 because, as you know by now, I value theopoetics. I also think that because theopoetics are interested in questions of construction—how is God made (*poesis*)?—this psalm, like the Exodus 2 story, offers us symbols and language for *making* sense of a God-in-the-making who is coming to be in response to a world he takes responsibility for. God, we might say, is his respons(ibility) to an Other. (Which is a claim systematic theology can explain in terms of the doctrine of the trinity: God is his being-for others, that is, the Father is Father in respect to the Son.)

I don't want to say, though, that God, in Jack's words, "empties without remainder into our God-talk." God does certainly empty himself, but never to the point at which God ceases to god. When we are talking of God, we are thinking of remainder, of more, et cetera. God is that in excess of *is*, that beyond that. God empties, but he empties both from and into his fullness. (Which is a claim systematic theology shouldn't try to explain.)

Theopoetics, like theology, can only do what it does with language (defined as broadly as you want: sign language, music, doodles). And language is metaphorical. It points beyond itself. I am not thinking of a facile distinction between a sign (d-o-g) and the signified (that fluffy, barking thing over there), but rather the excess of language that always eludes our attempts to capture it.

About a year into my relationship with Andy, I asked him *why* he loved me. He didn't have an answer. That afternoon, we visited Longwood Gardens, an exquisite, 1,110-acre botanical gardens in Kennett, Pennsylvania. We were watching bees buzzing around flowers, and I asked him to talk to me about pollination. Andy, a dentist, has a great way of breaking down scientific concepts, and I love listening to his jargon-free explanations. So, for the next ten minutes, the bees and flowers and I listened to Andy discuss this basic but complicated phenomenon. Later that night, when we were getting ready for bed, Andy told me he realized why he loved me. "When you asked me to talk to you about pollination, and we were there in the gardens for a few minutes together and I was answering your question. *That's* why I love you." Whatever he was communicating was *beyond* language, but he was using language to call attention to that fact. He was using language to tell me that language wasn't enough. That his love for me, communicated through language, lies nevertheless beyond its reach.

It is the same with our God-talk. If we are going to "get at" God, then we will have to do it with language. In his reflections on "God in human language," Cardinal Walter Kasper writes that "language contains a movement to transcendence. Not only can it, but it intends always to say more than what the factual case is."[20] *There is something going on in the name God*, and this going-on can be confessed *but not contained* in the name God. God always points to what is beyond God, and what is beyond God is God, a God who is always in the process of arising, always in the process of provoking us to watch for him to arise.

THREE

An Unlucky Cross

Did Jesus plan on being killed?

"For us the death of Jesus is, after all, a question put to God—to the God whom Jesus proclaimed."

—EDWARD SCHILLEBEECKX, *JESUS*

The work of Christian theology always begins underground, in a dark, musty tomb, with the body of a man whose death God didn't prevent. Yes, sure, the resurrection and all that—there's no Christianity without it! But the resurrection doesn't undo what precedes it. What is resurrected is a murdered body, and that body was murdered because God didn't prevent it from being murdered. All Christian theology must admit from go: God allowed his beloved son to be murdered.

If biblical theology had trouble making sense of God's faithfulness in a world-gone-wrong, then the crucifixion of Jesus drastically upped the stakes. If God had his eye on the downtrodden, then why allow

Jesus to be killed in this gruesome way? In fact, when Jesus, using the language of Psalm 22, asks why God has abandoned him, he positions himself among the orphans and widows that Psalm 82 sings about. "My God, my god, why have you forsaken me to the same fate suffered by all of those whose futures have been ripped away from them?" The cross is a spectacular failure—for Jesus, and for the God who abandons him.

Christians have traditionally tried to deal with this failure by arguing, well, actually, the cross was the plan all along. It didn't catch God or Jesus off guard, goes the argument. They both knew it was going to happen, and in fact *wanted* it to happen. See, for example, Anselm, who argued in *Cur Deus Homo* that Jesus's death satisfied humanity's sinful debt to God.[1] Jesus and God were in cahoots the whole time (save for a few minutes in the Garden of Gethsemane) to save humanity. Jesus had to die to satisfy his father's wrath against the sin that plagued humans ever since Adam and Eve took a bite of that fruit. The cross, therefore, wasn't a failure, or a going-wrong, but was precisely what the Father and Son (the Holy Spirit is usually missing from these theologies) set out to accomplish. This interpretation, to many laypeople, is often not understood as an interpretation but is instead seen as "the biblical perspective" on Christ's death.

One Easter while I was an undergraduate student at Liberty University, campus ministry hosted a showing of Mel Gibson's *The Passion of the Christ.* In addition to its antisemitic tone and historical inaccuracies, it's also incredibly and graphically violent—"torture porn," as a *Guardian* reviewer put it.[2] This, however, was the point, as one of our campus pastors reminded us after the film. "It's not that Jesus died, but that he died *like this*, enduring this amount of pain and brutality. And he did all of this *for you.*" We were then invited to stick around for a few minutes and thank Jesus for suffering on our behalf. We weren't primarily grateful for his life or his ministry or his love, but for his *brutal suffering.*

Now, however, this interpretation leaves me unsettled, queasy even. God's best plan to save the world involved murdering an innocent paragon of virtue, sending his only begotten son to die a cruel death? There were no better options? God is infinitely creative and had eternity to brainstorm—and *this* is the best he could come up with?

Contemporary theologians have pointed out the problems with this reading of the cross, namely that it drains the cross of what makes it the cross. Crucifixion in the ancient world, writes Morna D. Hooker:

> was an utterly gruesome form of business—a cruel and sadistic form of execution . . . described [by Josephus] as 'the most wretched of deaths.' . . . The scandal of the cross thus was not simply that Jesus had been put to death as a criminal, but that the particular death he had suffered was the most barbaric that could be devised.[3]

Various thinkers and artists over the years have tried to recapture some of the cross's original horror by setting it alongside contemporary terrors that we know well about. Catholic priest William Hart McNichols created a piece of art called AIDS Crucifixion, which depicted a lesion-riddled Jesus dying in front of a man holding up a Bible. A sign above his head names his crimes: "AIDS, HOMOSEXUAL, FAGGOT, PERVERT, SODOMITE."[4] And in *The Cross and the Lynching Tree*, James Cone allows both trees to interpret each other to encourage Christians to "face the cross as the terrible tragedy it was."[5]

> As Jesus was an innocent victim of mob hysteria and Roman imperial violence, many African Americans were innocent victims of white mobs, thirsting for blood in the name of God and in defense of segregation, white

> supremacy, and the purity of the Anglo-Saxon race. Both the cross and the lynching tree were symbols of terror, instruments of torture and execution, reserved primarily for slaves, criminals, and insurrectionists—the lowest of the low in society.[6]

These and other contemporary engagements with Calvary not only reconfront us with the horrific devastation of the event; they also remind us that these deaths should not have happened in the first place.

What, then, are we to do with the Nicene Creed, which tells us "For our sake [Jesus] was crucified under Pontius Pilate?" Or Paul's refrain that Christ "died for our sins" (1 Cor. 15:3, Rom. 5:8, 2 Cor. 5:21)? The Christian tradition is clear: Jesus died for our sins. His death *did something* and *means something* for us and our salvation. But as Paul also notes in his first letter to the Corinthians, there is a difference between "the mystery of God" that we proclaim "in lofty words or wisdom" and the crucified Jesus (I Cor. 2:1-2). There is the event itself, and then there are our attempts at making meaning from the event. These are not the same thing.

There is, of course, no such thing as a meaningless event; to experience a moment is to interpret it.

There is obviously no uninterpreted cross. In fact, the cross exists as a punishment in Rome *because of* its meaning. If Rome wanted someone dead, they would've killed him—but if they crucified him, it's because they both wanted him dead, and they wanted his death to mean something. All of which is to say that a Roman cross is always already in the process of being interpreted. Christians didn't give the cross meaning; they gave it new meaning—what they believed was *God's* meaning. So while we should keep in mind that the New Testament is working hard at interpreting the event of Jesus's death, we should remember that the only "events" the New Testament writes about are interpreted events. An uninterpreted cross does not have any place in Christian history.

We proceed, therefore, under the weight of a tension: between the crucifixion and the crucifixion *for us*. In both instances, where we start is the cross. God has revealed himself in this cross, and we cannot do Christian theology or theopoetics without it. As Moltmann put it: "When the crucified Jesus is called 'the image of the invisible God,' the meaning is that THIS is God, and God is like THIS."[7] This isn't to collapse all theology to Christology: It is to admit that as a Christian, Jesus is my point of entry to the divine. All my theological roads wind through Golgotha.

So we point to and start with and think from the cross. But this immediately presents us with a challenge. As Fleming Rutledge points out in a brilliant book that grapples honestly with the crucifixion, "the great church councils that succeeded in defining the nature of Christ and the Holy Trinity left us with no equivalent conciliar definition of the cross."[8] This echoes Wolfhart Pannenberg's insight that the Apostles' Creed displays an "astonishing sobriety" when it comes to explaining the theoretical significance of the crucifixion. "Only the sequence of events is expressly mentioned—none of the early Christian interpretations of the death of Jesus."[9] Such credal silence, Rutledge suggests, grows from the early Christian belief that the cross "favors a multifaceted understanding rather than favoring one theory over against another."[10] If the cross is to be understood, it must be interpreted. Its "significance … is not self-evident." The cross "does not easily explain itself."[11]

Nor does the New Testament explain it. In fact, the New Testament is not, on the whole, too systematic about the meaning and accomplishment of the cross. To even get at what God is up to with the cross, the writers take up theopoetics. They begin to think about God in terms of what they've learned from their sacred texts. Jesus's death was sacrificial; he is our lamb. He gave his life to pay a ransom; he is our redeemer. And on and on the early Christians went trying to make sense of the monstrously incomprehensible: that Jesus, their Lord, was murdered on a Roman cross.

We all know what it's like to have our words fail us when tragedy strikes. Even the most eloquent among us have trouble doing philosophy in the wake of horror. But silence is usually not an option; even if we refrain from talking out loud, our internal self-talk is unrelenting. Our spouse has a heart attack and although we have the explanation (the heart attack), we need more, especially if we're religiously inclined. I've seen people grope for this *more* in real-time as they try to make sense of devastation. So, for instance, we say that our spouse's heart didn't just give out, but that God loved him so much that he couldn't bear to be without him in heaven. Or we say that our spouse actually *chose* to go be with God in a different world, or as the bereavement rhetoric puts it, "a better place." One of my young cousins told me that our recently departed aunt could fly because she became an angel. Church friends at funerals assure me that "God's ways are not our ways" and that he has a plan even though we can't currently see it.

Most of these images make my skin crawl, but when I sit with them, I realize there is a kernel of theological truth in each one. God *does* love my friend's spouse and has always desired to be with him. Many people *do* assent to their deaths, willingly trusting their lives to God as they exhale into his eternity. My aunt, who spent her life weighed down by resentments and unfair trials, no doubt *is* whizzing about in some new existence unmoored by the physical and emotional gravities of her past life. And of course, God's ways are mysterious and inscrutable, and we can't predict what he'll do next. It might take some work on our part to bring the theological insights to the foreground, but they are already there, bubbling up in the images.

We have to be careful, though, to remember that even good images are images *of* whatever event they are imaging. Our theologies of the crucifixion are not the crucifixion. There is much more going on in that event than we can put into words. If we don't keep this distance in mind—the gap between the event and our reflections on and portrayals of the event—then our theology will be impoverished. Better to let the images run free, to give them room to play, room to flirt with us and each other, to goad us into experiencing the elusive divine "with sighs too deep for words" (Rom. 8:26).

Jesus's earliest followers can lead the way, as Kallistos Ware points out:

> If we look in the New Testament, what we find is not a single way of understanding the saving work of Christ, not a single systematic theory of salvation, but we have whole series of images, and symbols set side by side. They are symbols of profound meaning and power, yet for the most part they are not explained but left to speak for themselves. If we want to understand the work of Christ, it is better to follow what the New Testament does and to have a number of different images in our mind. We should not isolate any single image of Christ's work, but we should combine them together. Our best motto is: safety in numbers.[12]

And so, as troubling as these images can be to our modern sensibilities, we must let them all be, we must confess them all in our liturgies and prayers: sacrifice, ransom, Christus Victor, et cetera. But we must remember—always, always remember—that what these images are *of* is a moment in time when the world went horrifically wrong.

Let's start there: The cross wasn't supposed to happen.

When the World Went Very Wrong

Jesus was killed by Rome. This is beyond dispute. Why he was killed is a different matter, and plenty of historians have attempted an answer. There is, however, another question that is often overlooked: Why weren't Jesus's followers killed? This is a line of inquiry that Paula Fredriksen pursues in her book *Jesus of Nazareth, King of the Jews*.[13] If Jesus was really a threat to Rome (as other crucified individuals were believed to be), then his entire movement would have been shut down decisively. He would've been crucified alongside his followers. For that matter, if he was truly a threat to the ruling authorities, Jesus would have been stopped long before he was, just like his predecessor John the Baptist.

But Jesus, for the most part, was allowed to preach at will. He was given freedom to move throughout Galilee. Why didn't the state intervene? They didn't believe they had to. His teachings (turn the other cheek, don't retaliate) do not smack of insolence directed at civil authorities. His message of radical love and forgiveness does not seem particularly antagonistic other than to those whose Bible readings have been influenced by a subtle antisemitism: as if Jesus's Jewish contemporaries would be offended by his "radical" suggestion that God is loving and forgiving.

So if Jesus wasn't really a threat, why was he crucified? Fredriksen offers an explanation that manages to make more sense of the historically agreed-upon data than other popular explanations of Good Friday. Breaking from scholars and turning her critical eye on John's Gospel, Fredriksen assumes that Jesus and his followers moved freely between the Galilee and Judea throughout their ministry. Such trips included visits to Jerusalem, likely on pilgrimage days when crowd turnout was at its highest. Because passions tended to flare up on holidays, civil and religious authorities kept a watchful eye on everything that happened, especially in the Temple. This is how they knew Jesus's message "was in no practical way revolutionary."[14] But on what would be his last visit to the Temple, something went wrong, claims Fredriksen. "Jesus evidently lost control of his audience," she says.[15] Here is how the chips might have fallen:

> The chief priests know what Pilate knows: Jesus himself is not dangerous. But for the first time, this Passover, the crowds who swarm around him are. In the intensity of their expectation—that the Kingdom was literally about to arrive? That Jesus was about to be revealed as messiah? That the restoration of Israel was at hand?—they are restive, potentially

> incendiary. The chief priests are the ones so positioned to know both the temperament of the holiday crowd, and—because they share a common tradition—the disruptive potential of a lively messianic expectation.[16]

If anything went wrong with the festive pilgrims, the chief priests had Rome to answer to. And so, they alerted Pilate, who knew what to do. Arresting Jesus would be easy; he was, after all, notoriously nonviolent; there would be no struggle. He'd be arrested at night and crucified before sunup. "Let [the crowds] wake up to their messiah already on a cross. . . . Killing Jesus publicly, by crucifixion, would go a long way toward disabusing the crowds"[17] of their messianic zeal. Perhaps, Fredriksen suggests, the Last Supper tradition contains a trace of this retelling: Jesus realized he'd lost control of his message and gathered his followers together for what he suspected might be their final mcal.

Fredriksen's book has received its fair share of criticism. Her reconstructions are firmly grounded in her own scholarly research, but they are nevertheless speculative. Steven M. Bryan wonders whether Fredriksen makes too much of the Passover crowds: "Is it really so hard to suppose that a messianic claim by or for Jesus was viewed as potentially dangerous and that in the absence of an organized mass response to Jesus . . . the Roman authorities became convinced that his death would preemptively defuse any threat created by his rising popularity?"[18] And John R. Donahue, S.J., suggests Fredriksen doesn't give enough consideration to other explanations for the disciples' survival: that they were lucky enough to escape arrest.[19] For my own part, I've got several disagreements, not least of which is that I happen to believe some state actors might have been uncomfortable with some of Jesus's kingdom talk. (See, for instance, how flustered some American politicians get when people remind them of Jesus's instructions to become a neighbor to everyone who crosses your path, a category which surely includes both the undocumented and those who are afraid of them.) On the whole, however, while I don't have the history chops to adjudicate Fredriksen's hypothesis, I think the story she tells is compelling—historically *and* theologically. What I love about her work is that it takes the cross seriously *as a cross.* In Fredriksen's reading, Jesus's murder is really a murder. It is an actual, flesh-and-blood going-wrong. Perhaps Jesus realized at some point that his murder was likely, and perhaps he often entertained the possibility that he, like other prophets, would meet an early demise. But that doesn't change the fact that Jesus's murder was an accident, a chance occurrence, an extremely unfortunate happening in a world that seems to go ever wrong.

A New Starting Point for Theologies of the Cross

But how can we do meaningful Christian theology from an accidental cross? Let's start by turning the question around: How can we do meaningful Christian theology from a *planned* cross? Planned by whom? God? For what reason? So that he could be allowed to forgive humans? Allowed by whom? What standard for forgiveness is there beside God himself? Further, why does someone have to die for God to forgive human sin? Can't he just . . . choose to forgive us? As Elizabeth Johnson has noted, any crucifixion theology that presupposes that God's forgiveness can only be granted after he extracts a penalty does *not* take seriously Jesus's own teachings on forgiveness (that is, that we ought to forgive people easily and eagerly).[20]

When I discuss the crucifixion with Catholic students, they instinctively latch onto the atonement theories they grew up hearing in church: Jesus died for our sins, Jesus's sacrifice satisfied God's wrath, et cetera. One day, I asked a young man if he wanted to have children. When he told me he did, I asked him to imagine that one day his son stole something.

"Would you let your son's actions slide or would you hold him accountable for his wrongdoing?" I asked. "I would definitely hold him accountable," my student replied. "And how would you do that?" I pressed. "Would you make him return what he stole and then send him to his room, or would you, in the interests of justice, have somebody murdered?"

Some might dismiss this line of reasoning as overly facile. "God is more complicated than that!" But Jesus doesn't think so. In fact, Jesus tells us, in quite simple terms, that Jesus is like a good father who wants us to be happy, who delights in our requests for good things. "Is there anyone among you who, if your child asked for bread, would give a stone?," asks Jesus, "Or if the child asked for a fish, would give a snake? If you then, who are evil, know how to give good gifts to your children, how much more will your Father in heaven give good things to those who ask him" (Matt. 7:9–11).

We have to be careful labeling the discomforting conclusions of our theology as "mysteries." This isn't to say that there aren't any mysteries in the Christian life. There are! The First Vatican Council declared anathema anyone who believed that divine revelation "contained no true mysteries" and that "all the dogmas of the faith can be understood and demonstrated by properly trained reason from natural principles."[21] But to claim that Jesus was sacrificed and that this sacrifice pleases God is already to leave the realm of mystery and to enter the world of reasoning and explanation. It won't do to pretend that God thinks we are wise enough to understand that his justice requires blood, but not wise enough to understand why that requirement exists in the first place.

Although he sometimes claimed otherwise, C. S. Lewis was clearly up to "explaining"—in his unmatched literary way, to be sure—substitutionary atonement in his novel *The Lion, the Witch, and the Wardrobe.* The story concerns the Pevensies children—Peter, Susan, Edmund, and Lucy—who entered a snowy wood by way of a wardrobe. This world had been enchanted by the White Witch, whose spell had forced it to endure a brutal (and Christmas-less) hundred-year-long winter. Fearful of an ancient prophecy that said her rule will be ended by four humans, the Witch plots to kill the children, starting with Edmund. He was a traitor, she reasoned, because he was willing to bring his siblings to her in exchange for Turkish delight. "You know that every traitor belongs to me as my lawful prey and that for every treachery I have a right to a kill," she tells Aslan the lion.[22] In Narnian rhetoric, this requirement is owed to a mystery called "Deep Magic."

Aslan strikes a deal with the Witch, and she agrees to take his life in exchange for Edmund's. But though the Witch knew the Deep Magic, she had no idea about the deeper magic, which holds that "when a willing victim who had committed no treachery was killed in a traitor's stead, the Table would crack and Death itself would start working backward."[23]

Narnian fan though I am, I do wish Lewis had been more careful about forming children's imaginations with the rhetoric of redemptive violence. Although Narnia is fictional, the logic of the Deep Magic is remarkably similar to popular Christian interpretations of the cross: Just as Aslan had to die in Edmund's place, Jesus *had to die* in our place. There was no other way to go about it. I suppose, though, the big question to ask of this Deep Magic (Narnian or Christian; either is more fantastical than the next) is why it exists in the first place. Did God create this standard? But why would a God of love create such a standard? Perhaps some might argue that the Deep Magic preexists God; but then we run into the thorny theological problem of separating God from justice, and that isn't going to get us very far. So if there is Deep Magic, then the magician must be responsible for it. But all my theological sensibilities lead me to believe that a God of love and justice would never create a world that was redeemable only via murder.

Fredriksen may well be right that our crucifixion narratives don't make the best historical sense. But to me, they don't make good *theological* sense, as Joseph Ratzinger (later Pope Benedict XVI), points out. "Many devotional texts actually force one to think that Christian faith in the cross imagines a God whose unrelenting righteousness demanded a human sacrifice, the sacrifice of his own Son, and one turns away in horror from a righteousness whose sinister wrath makes the message of love incredible."[24] Indeed! A planned cross turns God into a murderer, robs Jesus of his victimhood, and consecrates violence. If God the Father can force his son to suffer torture, then what is wrong with an earthly father beating his son for good reason? If God the Loving redeems the world by way of state violence, then surely the death penalty can have a positive effect on society. The idea of redemptive violence animates a good deal of our popular culture. Soldiers don't die senseless and preventable deaths: They give their lives as sacrifices on behalf of their countries. People don't randomly develop cancer: God sends it to them so they might learn a valuable lesson from their suffering. Societies don't improve unless people are punished—and sometimes killed—for their crimes. And a justified cross, justified by God, justifies all of it.

When I was growing up and learning how to "lead people to Jesus" (that is, convert them to Christianity), we were told that we could sum up the entire Christian faith in the words of John 3:16 (KJV): "For God so loved the world, that he gave his only begotten Son, that whosoever believes in him shall not perish, but have everlasting life." By "gave," we understood John to be saying "gave up to be murdered." But does this act really reveal a God of infinite love?

Perhaps there are better ways to understand what John is trying to convey to his readers: Because God loves the world, God gives it Jesus. Jesus's crucifixion happens not because of what God intends (that is, to give us a gift) but because of how the world responds (that is, by rejecting God's gift). God doesn't give Jesus to the world so Jesus can die, but so that the world (perhaps for the first time in its four-and-a-half-billion year history) can *live*, and live "abundantly" and "eternally."

The Cross: A Spectacular Failure

"No exception to perhaps the only ironclad rule in all of nature," writes Elizabeth Johnson, "Jesus died."[25] It is in fact this "ironclad rule of nature" that God in Jesus submits himself to, standing in solidarity with not only human life but *all flesh*. (As

Johnson also notes, *sarx* connotes "a broader reality" than human bodies.[26]) This interpretation of Jesus's life, death, and resurrection is called "deep incarnation," a theological idea popularized by Niels Henrik Gregersen. Here is how he defines it:

> "[D]eep incarnation" is the view that God's own Word (logos) and Wisdom (sophia) was made ordinary flesh in Jesus Christ in such a capacious manner that God, by assuming the particular life story of Jesus the Jew from Nazareth, also conjoined the material conditions of all creaturely existence ("flesh"), shared and ennobled the fate of all biological life forms ("grass" and "lilies"), and experienced the pains of sensitive creatures ("sparrows" and "foxes") from within. Deep incarnation thus presupposes a radical embodiment of the Son of God that reaches into the roots (radices) of material and biological existence as well as into the darker aspects of creation, from the breaking down of material structures to animal and human suffering.[27]

Jesus's incarnation is deep, in other words, because by taking on flesh, he plunges down into the very depths of the evolutionary universe, thus joining "in solidarity with all creatures' living and dying through endless millennia of evolution, from the extinction of species to every sparrow that falls to the ground."[28] The atonement, then, should be understood as at-*one*-ment, the phenomenon of God's becoming inextricably united with the world he has created, a world in which all living things eventually die.

I find a lot of merit in this interpretation of the cross, but it might, at least the way I read it, risk distracting us from the cross's cruelty. The cross doesn't declare that God stands with all life as it passes away into nothingness, but that he stands with certain lives as they are wickedly snuffed out. If God wanted to stand in solidarity with living beings as they pass from life to death, then he could have demonstrated this to us by becoming a human who died a natural death. The crucifixion pushes beyond this by calling our attention to a God who stands in solidarity with the unlucky. Or, more to the point, a God who stands in solidarity with the world even *as it blatantly insists on going wrong*. Moltmann reminds us of this important difference when he writes, "In Jesus he does not die the natural death of a finite being, but the violent death of the criminal on the cross, the death of complete abandonment by God. The suffering in the passion of Jesus is abandonment, rejection by God, his Father."[29]

The trouble with explaining the cross consists in *explaining the cross*. We can make theological meaning *from* the cross, but this means making meaning after the fact. This means going to Golgotha, crawling up trembling to the cross, and wondering how the Holy One of God could ever become this mutilated pile of rotting flesh. I once gently pushed back against my friend's claim that God had sent brain cancer to a father in her community. After his death, his wife became very involved in local fundraising efforts for brain cancer research, raising tens of thousands of dollars for different medical organizations. "I know what you mean about God not being responsible for his death," my friend told me, "but when you see all the good that came out of it, it's hard to believe that God didn't want that to happen."

No doubt the woman whose husband died of brain cancer has responded to grief in creative, productive ways. She has found a way to make her late husband's life and death matter, to make them mean something. God, of course, takes joy in this kind of human goodwill. But this doesn't mean God intended for anyone to die of brain cancer; it means that we, just like God, are meaning-making people. Tragedy is unplanned; our *responses* to tragedy, at least after the initial shock wears off, are often carefully planned.

It is the same with Jesus's cross. To say that God was up to something in the event of the crucifixion is not to say that God planned on it happening, or worse, that God wanted it to happen. All we are saying is that once it happened, God decided to happen, too, and to happen as only he can. In the next chapter, we will discuss the resurrection, without which the crucifixion would not mean much. In fact, if Jesus had not been resurrected, it's unlikely that anyone would have spent time trying to make meaning from the cross. The Easter Christ is who he is because of the cross; equally as important, the crucified Jesus is who he is because the Spirit eventually announces him to be the risen Lord. Both events interpret each other, mean what they do only through the other.

And yet: We must keep in mind that the cross is not simply a precursor to the empty tomb. Easter Sunday is not the logical outcome of Good Friday. The one doesn't lead to the other the way A leads to B. What God does to Jesus after his death is unexpected. When I was growing up in a Pentecostal church, I used to often hear, usually in response to something terrible happening, that "Sunday's on the way!" Tragedy was not appreciated *as such* but was seen only as the stuff out of which God performs miracles. We are the spectators, God is the magician, and the bad thing that happened to us is one of his rigged cards, a mere prop designed to help him pull off a trick and win our admiration. May we never allow the cross to be interpreted in this petty way. Sunday does come, of course; but not as an end. Sunday begins something truly new. Friday never, ever leads to it.

Our task, then, is to look at this Friday corpse—a corpse that is, if I had to wager a guess, not convinced that Sunday's on the way—and to wonder how God might be present to this dead man.

The presence of God in this pile of bleeding flesh *is* the cornerstone of the gospel. Which is why we ought to be skeptical of some of the popular interpretations of the crucifixion. Whether we say that Jesus was sacrificing himself to God or paying our ransom to God, we are doing exactly what the New Testament won't let us do—removing God from the side of the murdered victim. Whatever God was doing when Jesus was dying on a tree, he was doing it *in Jesus*. "God was *in Christ*, reconciling the world unto himself" (2 Cor. 5:19, KJV, emphasis added). Jesus might have felt abandoned by God in his hour of suffering, but God was intimately present to him, however hidden he might have been from the person gasping for air. Jesus did not die without God; he died *into* God. And the Father somberly accepted him. If the language of sacrifice is meaningful at all, it must keep front and center the conviction that God received Jesus as someone whose pure life did not warrant its cruel end.

God accepts Jesus as a victim of history. God does not stop Jesus's death but embraces it—embraces it not as a prelude to the resurrection, but as a summing up of the tragic history of humanity. A history where the world's forgotten die miserable deaths due in no small part to the failures of their governments and the communities that are charged with protecting them. Jesus, as victim, recapitulates to God the history of the world's orphans and widows, a history of the neglected, of society's leftovers. And God accepts it. Perhaps when he does so, he acknowledges his own failure. If only he'd arisen the way his people believed he could. But no—the cross of Jesus doubles down on the challenge of Psalm 82, and God, receiving the corpse of his beloved, finally accepts defeat. The world has gone horribly wrong. So God holds his beloved son to his chest, and simultaneously mourns a history of tragedy while dreaming of a future that might redeem it.

Jesus Died for Us?

The Church has always held that Jesus's death was for us. In his first letter to the Corinthians, Paul quotes a credal formula that he received: "Christ died for our sins in accordance with the scriptures" (1 Cor. 15:3). Yes and amen. *And*, I insist, this death was the result of a confluence of unlucky factors. How can we square both these beliefs? That Jesus's unplanned death is in any way *for us*? Let's take a stab at it.

We need to start by being clear about Jesus's vocation, without which we would not be able to offer a coherent vision of the cross. Jesus's life consisted of his complete openness to God and to the world. In Craig Keen's words, "He is the open place where all that God is participates in all that we are that all that we are may participate in all that God is."[30]

Jesus did not *intend* to die on the cross, if by that we mean he planned on it. But his life, his way-of-being in a world that insists on going wrong, that insists on contributing to its own going-wrong, *stretched* (*tendere*) toward a wretched end. When I say that Jesus's death was accidental, I don't mean that it came out of the blue. There were signs he would meet with doom, but none of these signs seemed to thwart him from his vocation. Jesus lived his life with an unflinching faithfulness to God and God's cause, a faithfulness that remained steadfast even in the face of death. I'll let Edward Schillebeeckx make the point:

> That someone like Jesus, who was proclaiming the imminent arrival of God's rule, would

> have failed to ponder, in some way, so probable and to him so clearly recognizable an outcome of his future life, can be ruled out from the start. It would mean that Jesus's end was in flagrant contradiction to what he had himself been saying about having a radical confidence in God. . . . Thus, the fact of his approaching death was something that Jesus was bound to integrate into his overall surrender to God.[31]

Although I believe strongly that the crucifixion was not God's plan, Jesus almost certainly knew that crucifixion, and death in general, was one of Rome's plans. And it was precisely this kingdom of death—more to the point, *all* kingdoms of death, all kingdoms that achieve and maintain power through the power and threat of death—that Jesus was protesting. Everything about his life, every moment of his ministry, the way he welcomed all without precondition to God's table, the way he joyfully embraced those society deemed unembraceable—these are the actions of the enfleshed Word that says NO to every NO that has ever been sounded in human history. Jesus is God's YES to a world-gone-wrong, a YES to its potential, to its promise. Surely Jesus had a feeling that the wrongness he was protesting on God's behalf might one day overtake him. No matter. He would continue to sing and to *be* God's YES to the world, to embrace the whole universe as a creation that has forgotten that God has eternally declared it good. In his living or in his dying, he would be *for* others.

This for-ness is the key to all Christian interpretations of the cross. Jesus, said Dietrich Bonhoeffer, is who he is by virtue of who he is for. He takes his being from us, from the world that he lives for, the world that he dies for. To believe the latter claim isn't to play the dead-end game of "reconstructing" Jesus's psychology as he went to the cross. It is merely to believe, with Bonhoeffer, that the ground of Christ's divinity is his "being there for others," which he "maintained till death."[32] Jesus may not have planned his fate, but he accepted it nonetheless. He did not put up a fight, but rather, as the Gospels make clear, went willingly to his death. Jesus consented to tragedy as it befell him, poured out his life even as it was ripped from and beaten out of the body that he had always offered to everyone he encountered. "This is my body," Jesus tells his disciples during their final meal together, perhaps having puzzled out that his end was near. Not just any body, but a body *for you*. A body constituted by the others for which it offers itself, in life and death. A body that is completely turned out, turned toward the world. A body that totally, unreservedly loved and loved hard and loved without end even to the end.

And now we can start to reflect on the second part of the formula: that Jesus died not only *for* us, but for *our sins*. As usual, when it's talking about "sin," scripture deploys a range of images and concepts to say what it wants to say. Transgression, impurity, rebellion, debt, fall—all of these are different ways of saying not simply that the world has gone wrong, but that the world has gone wrong and that humans don't seem to care (and even if they did, they couldn't fix it on their own initiative). Sin is not a thing; it's a process. Sin happens when relationships break down, when the world doesn't *world* the way it's supposed to, the way God wants it to, when the world doesn't live up to its own promise, the promise that God gifted to it when he told the light to come be. James Keenan, S.J. defines sin as "the failure to bother to love," which is probably the best way to put it.[33] To sin is to fail to love the world that happens to you because you are so turned in on the individual worlding that you are. Of this sin, Jesus was surely innocent.

On the cross of Jesus, God intimately unites himself with a world-gone-wrong, a world shut up in itself, a world closing ever in on itself. God reconciles the world to himself by standing in solidarity with all those the world has failed to love, as well as all of those who fail to love. When scripture says, God "made him to be sin who knew no sin" (2 Cor. 5:21), it means to say that on the cross Jesus himself, the love of God incarnate, experiences the world's failures of love.

"Having loved his own who were in the world," writes John, "he loved them to the end" (John 13:1). To the *telos*, the goal at which he aimed throughout his life. As he moved throughout Galilee, bringing God's kingdom to all who wished to receive it, he remained razor-focused on his telos. Like an archer with his sights fixed on his mark, Jesus single-mindedly pursued his goal, which was the realization of God's kingdom, a kingdom of love, of peace, of neighborliness, a kingdom where all are turned out to the world and ready to embrace the world as it happens to them. Jesus's goal was to bring about God's rule, God's reign, not a different world, but a different worlding of the world we've already got.[34] Jesus longed for the world to world in accordance with the promise that God frontloaded it with. From this, Jesus did not waver. Love was his means and his end. From the moment of his baptism, he shot through the world like a pebble masterfully flung from a slingshot at its goal. He never "missed his mark," never sinned.

His crucifixion, however, casts a giant question mark across his mission. If he didn't waver from his target, he was nevertheless unsuccessful in hitting it, not because of his aim but because of unforeseen obstacles. His relentless pursuit of the passionate love of God was ended prematurely by the corrosive and abusive powers of hate that seem to have free reign in this world. This is also where we can begin to make sense of the *for-ness* of Jesus's death. Like all of those who die while waiting for their dreams to be fulfilled, Jesus died with unrealized hopes. In his cry "Why have you forsaken me?" is implied a darker question: Why have you forsaken *all the forsaken?* Jesus's death is *for us*, for those of us who will, forsaking our dreams, die before we want to. He collects our agonies *for* the purposes of hurling them at God.

This saying, which Matthew and Mark place on Jesus's lips, comes from Psalm 22, which seems to have been in the minds of those who first remembered and circulated the crucifixion stories. All four Gospels, for instance, narrate the Roman soldiers casting lots for Jesus's clothing, deliberately echoing Psalm 22:18 (ESV), "they divide my garments among them, and for my clothing they cast lots." In fact, the Gospels take up several psalms and put them to new use in their telling of the Jesus story. As I bring this chapter to a close, I'd like to follow their lead and think through the crucifixion alongside Psalm 82.

If you recall, Psalm 82 narrates a history of God, how he became The One God by out-loving every other god in the pantheon. The other gods overlooked the down-and-out in their charge, failed to take responsibility for them. So God, the one who becomes The One God, judges them for their failures, strips them of their deity, and takes their nations into his estate. His response is to become responsible for the forsaken of the earth. He *is* only as he takes responsibility for them. His very being is constituted by his concern for the orphans and widows. If he stops being concerned for them, he will suffer the same fate as the deities whose death the psalm narrates. This is why his worshippers *must* call on him to arise on behalf of the world: He comes to be as he comes to arise. If he does not arise, well, the show's over. Psalm 82 sums up the theological challenge writ large throughout the Hebrew Bible: The world has gone wrong, God needs to act, why isn't he?

The crucifixion narratives take up this challenge, but answer it in a surprising way: The world has gone wrong, God needs to act, *and he is*. Behold! The man hanging dead on a tree: God's act.

This isn't substitutionary atonement but participatory at-one-ment. Jesus doesn't switch places with us humans but joins us, becomes *one* of us, unites himself to our despair, subjects himself to a world that goes wrong, to a world that twists and hiccups down paths blazed open by accidents, misfortunes, and luck, both bad and good. The world is full of orphans and widows, of the overlooked and neglected, of the poor and needy, of the downtrodden. And God, rather than arising on their behalf—perhaps, even, realizing that he can't, for whatever reason—plunges down into their very misfortune. The Son of God becomes an orphan. The beloved of God finds himself widowed.

The cross of Jesus mocks a God who does not arise on behalf of the world. And God, bowing his head, accepting the protests of his suffering world, lies down on a cross and—*how unlucky!*—dies.

FOUR

Resurrection

Laughter after death

"There is no danger at the end of the world he will not know where to find me and raise me up."
—St. Monica, Augustine's mother, *Confessions*

Last fall, when our friend Carl died, Andy and I spent time with his wife and daughters, our godchildren. As we explained to the oldest, then two and a half years old, that her daddy was not coming home, we watched her little mind try to understand what we meant. She didn't, of course, get it right away; it had to sink in. It still does, nearly a year later. Sometimes she forgets and mentions her father, and we'll have to remind her that he's passed away. But we always, always insist that she will see daddy again.

Our goddaughters were baptized in the Catholic Church. Their parents and grandparents and godparents are all Catholic. We believe that the departed die into God, who receives them and takes responsibility for them. We believe in and look forward to the resurrection of the dead. We believe we will see Carl again.

On the day of the funeral, I assured Rusty, Carl's widow, that she would be reunited with her husband.

"I hope so," she told me through tears, making it sound as if she, a betting woman, were throwing all her chips on this one number.

"You will," I said, hoping for good luck. "We all will."

Like Rusty, I hope for resurrection. I believe that God is a god of resurrection. I am counting on it. I'm all in. But I'm not entirely sure about what this means. I know that our world is a world-gone-wrong, that it's full of death, that the history of the world is a history of death. Many of these deaths come about naturally. Many, like Jesus's, come about by cruelty. Each death, in its own way, introduces more agony and anguish to the world. And each throws the God of life into question.

One of the hymns sung at Carl's funeral was *Great Is Thy Faithfulness*, which celebrates God's constant, unwavering loyalty to the world.

> Summer and winter and springtime and
> harvest,
> Sun, moon, and stars in their courses above

join with all nature in manifold witness
to Thy great faithfulness, mercy, and love.[1]

How can we speak of God's faithfulness, though, in the land of the dead? How can we sing of his loyalty to us when, on his watch, those we love meet such abrupt, unexpected ends? To whom is he faithful? By what standards do we judge God faithful?

"Arise, O God," we've heard the psalm singers cry out. "Judge the earth!" We're counting on God to be the just, righteous, compassionate deity that he promises to be. But we sense he's not doing that. My goddaughters are orphans; their mother a widow. God did not arise to prevent Carl's heart attack.

In this book we've been talking about how we talk about God—including his power and his knowledge of the future. We decided that in the kind of world that we have, random luck plays a big role. God is not calling the shots, pulling the strings. He has not decided exactly what we will eat on Thursday and which politician will become the next president and when we will die. He couldn't make these decisions because (ignoring the apologist's theo-gymnastics) it's just not possible for God to know everything that will happen in a universe that unfolds according to open possibilities. Nor does he wield unlimited power: stepping in to prevent a heart attack, or to zap away a tumor, or to change the trajectory of a bullet are not abilities of his.

The resurrection of Jesus, however, *does* confront us with God's earth-shattering, death-smashing power, a power that does seem to be supernatural: God interferes with the natural course of events and causes Jesus, after his crucifixion, to once again come to be. What kind of power is this?

God's power consists in his power *to be* and *to be God* and *to be this* God. And *this God* is a god of life, a god whose very being consists in his eternal arising on behalf of the world that he takes responsibility for.

The answer to the question "What kind of God would allow this devastating thing to happen?" can only be: a god of resurrection.

In the following pages, we're going to reflect on resurrection, not systematically but theopoetically. In this, we will be following the lead of the first witnesses to the resurrection, who did not leave us metaphysical treatises on the event, but rather pieced together disparate, bizarre stories to construct a poetics of Easter. Our reflections aren't going to move logically from one to the next. There is nothing logical about resurrection.

Resurrection, joke-like, comes out of nowhere. It doesn't logically follow what comes before it. It is, like the best punchline, hysterically unpredictable.

You aren't counting on it. Jesus's followers certainly weren't, at least not like this. James G. Dunn refers to the "unexpectedness" of the early claims that Jesus had been raised. "Appearances of Jesus which impacted on the witnesses as *resurrection* appearances did not conform to any known or current paradigm. Instead, they created their own."[2] Sure, there were nascent theologies of martyrs swirling around, and yes, some Jews did look forward to a general resurrection. How else would God judge the dead? But one body rising before the general resurrection was not on anyone's radar. Perhaps not even on Jesus's.

What about God's?

The basic premise of this book is that in our world, things go very wrong, that they *actually* go very wrong, which means they haven't been planned to go the way they go. They are real events, real happenings, or rather mishappenings. Neither we nor God want them to happen. Jesus's unlucky death on a Roman cross emblematizes this tragic history of mishap, sums up the narrative of a world-gone-wrong and offers it to God in both praise and protest.

This isn't to deny God power, but to reformulate what we mean by God's power. God's power consists in his freedom—God might not have chosen Jesus's tragedy to happen, but he gets to choose how he will respond to it.

And—alleluia—he does.

With this view, God is no longer behind the scenes performing A History of the World like a puppet show. Instead, God is a person who responds freely to what happens *on his own terms*. Rome is free to make their own choices; so is God, and therefore Rome is on notice. God does not feel bound to respond to seriousness with his own seriousness. God can simultaneously be affected by the seriousness of the cross and choose to undertake an action that exceeds the seriousness of the moment. And that is what he does. God attends the funeral of Jesus, but he doesn't do so with a straight face. He cries, even as he reminds himself of one of Jesus's favorite sayings: that those who weep will laugh.

God comes to a tomb on Easter morning and, just like Jesus before the grave of Lazarus, laughs at all the unrealized possibilities that are just waiting to be activated. And then, as only the God of life can do, he activates them. He sees the potential in decay. He calls forth things that are not. He breaks his future ecstasy into a present sorrow. He mourns the corpse in front of him and invites him to be *more than dead*. And the dead body, recognizing the laughter of his Abba, begins to laugh as well: at first a bit restrained—quiet, demure, almost polite: his ribs, like his wounded hands, still sore—but soon, the laughter overtakes his entire corpse until he starts shaking, convulsing. And then cackling Spirit decides to take things even further and teases the corpse with an old joke: "Son of Man, can these bones live? Huh? Huh?" And the laughter in that tomb becomes excessive and deranged and lunatic because the dead bones joke is one of God's favorites. And all of a sudden, a group of mourning women are standing, confused, in a dark empty tomb, wondering what happened to their Lord's body.

This Same Jesus Whom You Crucified

Christian theology begins in a basement, in a tomb, in places of darkness, in moments of abandonment, of forsakenness. When someone's dead body is taken down from a monstrous cross and tossed inside of a tomb, this is when theology gets to work. Because it's here that theology discovers God getting to work.

God works in places and times we don't suspect he's working. This is one lesson of the empty tomb: God is with us in death. He does not stand apart from, maintain distance between himself and the dead, no matter how gruesome their departures. He is, even as they accuse him of abandonment, receiving them delicately, tenderly, like a mother who holds her baby to her breast one last time before his cremation. Love in the face of death: the soil from which resurrection springs.

This stronger-than-death love of God is the basis of any and all Christian hope. Unless God is in *that* disgusting tomb with *that* reviled corpse, then there is no reason to believe in the future. A history of hope—if I may borrow a formula from Jacques Derrida—begins with hopelessness.[3]

But this is not a natural history. Hope does not spontaneously emerge from hopelessness. Hope, rather, is an intrusion into business as usual. Hopelessness quite naturally follows from a tragic state of affairs; immense sorrow provokes hopelessness. But what provokes hope? To be sure, humans are optimistic creatures, and there are evolutionary advantages to this. But hope goes beyond mere optimism. Optimism tells us that our departed loved ones remain in our memories. Hope tells us that they are held securely by the God of the living and the dead.

The resurrection is a doing-to, not an undoing-of. The resurrection does not undo the murder that precedes it, but takes it up, transforms it into a completely new phenomenon. The resurrection transforms the cross without denying anything that makes it the cross in the first place. All the horror, the sheer terror, the agony that closed in tight on Jesus as his life was snuffed out prematurely—these are all still there in his Easter body. There is no woundless resurrected Christ, no glorified, scarless body. The gashes in his hands are eternal reminders that his suffering remains. "And between the throne and the four living creatures and among the elders," writes John in his apocalyptic vision, "I saw a Lamb standing as though it had been slain" (Rev. 5:6, ESV).

A word on bodies: Back in my apologetics days, I would argue forcefully that the body that came out of the tomb was the same body that went into it. I don't any longer believe that's true and the New Testament witness seems to contradict this belief. If the body was the exact same body, then why did no one recognize it until Jesus said, "Guys, look, it's really totally me"? Paul, too, while insisting that "this Jesus"—*this one right here, whom you saw and touched and ate with*—is the one whom God raised, nevertheless emphasizes that Easter Jesus is a different kind of being. He is not disembodied, but his body is different than it was previously. Scholars debate exactly what Paul means in 1 Corinthians 15 (and who even knows if Paul knows what he means; much of his theology is contingent, written in the moment, constructed to troubleshoot on the fly), but he's clear that bodies "of dust" are different than bodies "of heaven." The former earthly bodies are perishable: They are crucifiable. The latter spiritual bodies are imperishable: They exist perpetually in resurrection life.

What's important to the Gospels, and what they are crystal clear on, is that this Jesus who was killed is this Jesus who was raised by God. The body which came out of the tomb is the "body" of Jesus. His wounds: "wounds." The entire New Testament imagination is animated by the conviction that on Easter, God does not cancel out the cross, but transforms it into something more. "The cross."

"The Cross"

What is the difference between the cross and "the cross"? The answer is both simple and anything but. The difference consists in the quotation marks, which signal that there is something going on, something more than we thought, that something is happening in and to the cross, in and to the man hanging on it. "The cross" is not less than a cross, not something other than a cross, but something *more—how much more!*—than a cross.

I learned about the usefulness of quotation marks from camp, an aesthetic theory that was popularized in the United States thanks to Susan Sontag's 1964 essay "Notes on Camp."[4] Camp, writes Sontag, high prophet of the aesthetic, "sees everything in quotation marks."[5] Look over there, at Mary Lou's front yard, to the right of the hydrangeas, just above the—what is that?—garden gnome in blue sunglasses. See the pink flamingo? I do too. And so does camp: which means we are no longer looking at a pink flamingo but rather a "pink flamingo." Or let's say it this way: We are looking at its et cetera. By throwing quotation marks around a pink flamingo, we are saying that a "pink flamingo" is more than what it is, that its very being is constituted by its possibilities.

Camp sees in excess; its vision is generous, the quotation marks signaling that something is up, something we might have otherwise missed had we not been paying attention. Really paying attention. Camp is always paying attention, like Moses in the desert, who discovers God only after taking a second look at a burning bush.

When camp throws something in quotation marks, it refuses to take whatever it is as straight, refuses to take it on its own terms. To take something straight is to take it for what it is. Camp never, ever takes seriously a thing's to-be, preferring instead to focus on its to-become, as in "What potentials are swirling around here that everyone else is missing?" To throw a thing in quotation marks is to confess that its identity comes from the future; it is what it might be.

And hence: "the cross of Christ."

The cross is a good thing for camp to take up because, as Esther Newton discovered during her field research on female impersonators in America, camp is obsessed with death and decay and horror. The gay men she studied had a "tendency to laugh at situations that to [her] were horrifying or tragic."[6] I'm reminded of a gay friend who, after having been diagnosed with HIV, responded, "When life gives you AIDS, make lemonades!" In fact, camp adores a good AIDS joke, as David Halperin notes in *How to Be Gay*.[7] See, for instance, Robert Patrick's 1987 one-person, one-act play, *Pouf Positive*, which contains lines like "AIDS! Oh, doctor, thank God: I thought you said, 'Age!'"[8] and "when I think of how I got it, I can't complain."[9] Halperin also points to a magazine written by and for HIV-positive men called *Plagueboy*, which featured campy articles such as "Sex and the Single T-Cell." A similar publication, he notes, called *Diseased Pariah News*, found its own ways to make lemon-AIDS. One fictitious ad was taken out for AIDS Barbie's Malibu Hospice. Beneath a naked

Barbie covered in lesions ran the words "Compliment her on her slim, trim new figure!"[10]

David Halperin calls this "suffering in quotation marks."[11] The suffering is there; there is no denying the lesions. But in responding in this comical way to tragedy, camp "works to drain suffering of the pain that it also does not deny."[12] Don't be misled into thinking that camp is a way of dismissing anything serious. As Christopher Isherwood says, camp makes fun not of, but *out of* suffering.[13] Quotation marks are not written with erasers. You can only put quotation marks around something you affirm. "Pain" is not *not* painful—the quotation marks just signal that pain is not its own final word.

So with the crucifixion. Death speaks a real word over Jesus, and Jesus, and the Father he entrusts his life to, receive that word in all its horror. The punchline of the resurrection was gloriously delivered, but there is no amount of laughter that can mute Jesus's cries from the cross. He will forever be the man who publicly and loudly accused God of abandoning him into the hands of his murderers. Friday is not a prelude to Sunday. Resurrection, like camp, comes from the future, which means Sunday decides what Friday will be. But this is only from the perspective of Sunday. The early Christians emphasized that Jesus was dead for three days; in other words, he was *really*, *totally, completely* dead, and his followers, who deserted him when Rome flexed its hand, had no thought of what more could be going on in Jesus's death. Death was the end: It is finished. Full stop.

After Death

Punchlines have a retroactive effect. They transform that which precedes them. Some of the cleverest involve antanaclasis, a type of pun. Meaning *to bend back against*, antanaclasis occurs when a speaker or writer repeats a term but gives it a completely new meaning. To take a well-known example from Benjamin Franklin: "We must all hang together or most assuredly we shall all hang separately." The word "hang" has been thrown in quotation marks. At first, we thought old Dogood was talking about cooperation; he was really talking about murder. As with much wordplay, the effect is initially one of confusion: the listener is temporarily thrown off, stopped in her tracks. She was listening intently, contentedly on her way to a meaning, The Meaning, the one that was gradually lighting up at the end of a tunnel. Then suddenly: surprise! The jokester threw the word "with" in quotation marks and decided it meant more than we originally assumed. No longer does the first part of the sentence lead to the second part. It's actually the other way around. The end of the sentence transforms all that came before it. The pun has put the thing to new use, the quotation marks given it new life.

"Jesus has been crucified" functions in a similar way. When we first hear the claim, our hearts fall. Then suddenly, God takes "crucifixion" in a new direction, the direction of his future, where death has no sting.

Camp, pun-like, enjoys playing with what it finds—words, sentences, dead bodies—taking it up and jiggling it in its hands, the way Grandmom did with Yahtzee dice, until it starts to dance around in new patterns. Camp is dynamic, leaving nothing unsettled. Not even the past.

Laughter is a prophetic warning to history that it should check its arrogance: before God, even the past can be unsettled.

But does God *really* unsettle the past? Does he really do something to the crucified body of Jesus, or to the mind of the disciples? Aren't quotation marks all in our heads?

It won't do to talk about the resurrection as if it's a metaphor for something happening simply inside the disciples' hearts and minds. I'm discussing the resurrection with help from camp, but this doesn't mean the resurrection is simply a fun or clever rereading or recoding of the crucifixion. Whatever God did when he laughed the murdered Jesus into new life, God did it *to Jesus*. We might be talking about that action with the help of quotation marks, but resurrection is not simply a matter of punctuation.

I am working against those respectable interpretations of the resurrection that you might hear in a Religious Studies department, interpretations that take all resurrection talk to be metaphorical. "Yes, in a sense, he lives with us in our hearts, of course he does! But that has nothing to do with his body."

But the creeds have always insisted on the bodiliness of the raised Jesus. Sure, it behaved in ways we don't expect bodies to: It walked through walls, for example, and disappeared. But when the Gospels say that Jesus ate fish with his friends, when he stood next to a fire and was warmed by its glow, when he invited Thomas to caress—gently though, Thomas!—his wounds, the Gospels are telling us: *I know you have trouble believing this, but this Jesus we have been talking about, this same Jesus who was murdered by Rome, has been, well, there's no other way to say it, given back his body by God, only it's a new body. Well, we mean it's kind of the same but, well, more than what it was. We didn't believe it either. We still aren't sure what we experienced. But we know it was him, the one crucified by Rome. It's really, totally him—there's just more* him *than there was before!*

On Easter Sunday, God does something to Jesus, something that I am trying to get my mind around by thinking theopoetically about camp. God unsettles the logic of crucifixion. Usually murder ends in death. This time it ends in the end of the end. God sees the more in death, the et cetera in crucifixion, and raises his beloved son to new life so he can see it too. At the moment Jesus is raised, he becomes who he always was. And we beheld the glory as of the only begotten of the Father.

Jesus takes his being from the future. He *is* only in reverse. The question "who is Jesus?" can only be answered by pointing to his "cross," and then pointing to what comes next. (That something definitely *comes next* is the central conviction of Christianity.) The Christ of faith who is risen in the future is recognized as the Jesus of history who died in the past. Jesus is who he will be and who he will be is the Christ of God, who "when the fulness of time had come," was born of a woman (Gal. 4:4). His future is remembered and retrojected onto his past. Even the most trivial of his actions can only be gotten at from the vantage point of his resurrection. Jesus has always been the Christ he becomes.

Here is how Craig Keen, one of my favorite theologians, puts it:

> When the "whole fullness of deity is pleased to dwell" in the mutilated body of Jesus, it is not only the tissue just beginning to decompose in the tomb that is glorified and thus raised from the dead, but Jesus's entire life, every heartbeat and breath, every action and passion, every day and night. The deed of resurrection does not leave cause and effect intact, but exalts it all—and to such an extent that he, this Galilean peasant whom Rome treated so badly, is In the beginning with God . . . as God.[14]

The Gospels preserve accusations that the resurrection didn't really happen, but they don't preserve any traces of an accusation that says, "But why him? Why did God do it to Jesus?" What happened to Jesus made sense to them (and even to his enemies, whose voices are preserved in the Jesus tradition). The resurrection of Jesus placed God's stamp of approval on his entire life. Everything that Jesus is and was and said and performed congeal into the wobbly stability of divine personhood the moment God raises him from the dead.

"Thursday, Friday, Saturday, and Sunday," writes Craig Keen, referring to Holy Week, "everything depends on how these days face each other and thus come to make one event. Jesus' life as a whole is determined in this week."[15] The narrative of people walking with Jesus on the road to Emmaus completely unaware of who he really was might preserve in literary form the theological lightning flash that Easter Sunday brought about (Luke 24:13–35). Just as Jesus's followers recognize who he is after death, they recognize who he was before death.

The resurrection of Jesus was not only his vindication, but also a confirmation that he's more than what he is, which means that he was always more than what he was. The resurrection activated potentialities within Jesus—potentialities that were always there. The moreness of the cross revealed Jesus's own et cetera.

He was always, even when dying on a cross, the resurrection and the life. He was always, even when forsaken by God and abandoned in hell, the fullness of God's presence.

So we look at the cross of Jesus and we see "the cross," which doesn't undo the cross but goes beyond it. And this, we are told, is good news. To become aware of the quotation marks is to experience conversion. Once you see the dying Jesus in this way—once you see *this Jesus* as more than dead—you are forever changed. Your vision becomes warped, garbled, distorted. You see reality, the darkest, most distressing reality, both for what it is and what it might become. In fact, you see that it is already in the process of becoming what it might become.

I'll repeat (and I'll keep repeating): This way of seeing does not undo anything. The cross is still every bit as terrible as it always was. Neither the resurrection nor resurrection-vision ("camp," in my terminology) pretend that the gruesome isn't gruesome. All resurrection means is that the cross does not get the final say. Suffering will not have the last word.

Or else that's what we hope.

It should be clear at this point why what God did to Jesus is good news for the world: Because to those of us with eyes to see, the camps among us, the Easter event assures us that this world-gone-wrong has a future. God will one day take action. This world—the one that is decaying, that is warming, that is losing its biodiversity—will be raised to new life.

But what kind of life? What kind of world will the resurrected world be? Will each animal species that has gone extinct be brought back to planet Earth? Will God bring back every tree and blade of grass that has burned in a wildfire? There have been an estimated seventeen billion humans on planet earth.

Will every single one of them be raised? Will they return to their homes? To their neighborhoods? Or will God surprise them by granting them life in a new country, one that they always dreamed of visiting? Will they have their same vocations? Their same level of intelligence? Will they have the abilities and disabilities that marked them out in their first go-round? The more you press it, the more it sounds like a fairy tale; but it is nevertheless what many of us seem to hope for when we think about our and our loved ones' resurrection.

Rethinking Resurrection

Andy and I, along with Rusty and our goddaughters, believe God will raise Carl. And we believe this on the basis of what God did to Jesus. Jesus's resurrection implies Carl's. That's why Paul calls the risen Lord "the first-fruits of those who have died."

We all, like my goddaughter, hope to see our departed loved ones again. We hope to embrace them and to laugh with them and to snuggle with them by a warm fire. Does resurrection promise us that we can look forward to these experiences?

A few thoughts as we try and puzzle it out. First, we have to remember that Easter is good news *for the world*. We are merely one part of that world—an important part, to be sure, but one part nevertheless.

One first-century Jewish framework for making sense of Jesus's resurrection was a belief in the general resurrection of the dead. One person being raised ahead of all the others was not on anyone's Bingo card. That God acted on behalf of one person, Jesus, to raise him to new life did not mean the old belief was wrong: In fact, it meant it was right, but it had to be slightly revised to show that God was already at work! Jesus was the firstfruits of the new world that was breaking into this world, the new world that this world-gone-wrong was transforming into. The Easter hope, then, is still a hope *for the world*, a hope that bases itself on the belief that Jesus is the inauguration of resurrection life. Jesus was an individual and was raised as an individual, but this is good news for all of us *collectively*.

Christ died for *our* sins, writes Paul. *We* shall all be changed, he assures us, in the twinkling of an eye. "For since death came through a human being, the resurrection of the dead has also come through a human being; for as all die in Adam, so all will be made alive in Christ. But each in his own order: Christ the first fruits, then at his coming *those who belong to Christ*" (1 Cor. 15:21–23, emphasis added). Whatever Paul means by "resurrection," God does that in two steps: once for Jesus, and then once later for everything else—not just *humans*, but as he makes clear elsewhere, "the whole creation" (Rom. 8:18–23). So, yes, Carl will be raised: but he will be raised as a member of a *we*.

Second, we have to think critically about what we mean by "person." Although we in the West tend to see our individual selves as the center of everything, that is not the way the Christian imagination conceives of personhood. An individual does not properly exist; a person comes to be alongside and through another. To work through this concept with my students, I ask them to tell me who they think I am, and they usually generate the same list: teacher, spouse, child, uncle, godfather, friend, neighbor, et cetera. Suppose, I ask them, we start erasing these identities one by one until we've got nothing left? At that point, who am I? The point is there is no "me" apart from the relationships of care that I am always already entangled in. As Simone Weil puts it, "To say 'I' is to lie."[16]

Third, if we come to be through one another during our lives, we continue to come to be through one another *after* our lives. This is what memory is: My loved one lives on in me as long as I do. She endures because I do. But what happens to her when I die? Does she in some way live on through my living on in another? How about when that person dies? How far can we extend the original life?

Eventually every single one of us with the capacity to remember someone will die. What will happen to those memories?

This brings us to the fourth point. If survival, says Joseph Ratzinger (later Pope Benedict XIV), "from a purely human point of view can only become possible through [man's] continuing to exist in another," then the hope for immortality, for the eternal maintaining of loving relationship, can only be fulfilled by God. I'll let him make the point.

> We have seen so far that man has no permanence in himself and consequently can only continue to exist in another but that his existence in another is only shadowy and once again not final, because this other must perish, too. If this is so, then only *one* could truly give lasting stability: he who *is*, who does not come into existence and pass away again but abides in the midst of transience: the God of the living, who does not hold just the shadow and echo of my being, whose ideas are not just copies of reality. I myself am his thought, which establishes me more securely, so to speak, than I am in myself.[17]

God's love sustains us in life, and it sustains us in death: This is what resurrection hope is. God sustains the world, even while and when it passes away. God's relationship with the world does not end even as the world transforms into its next evolutionary phase. Matter is one phase in the world's evolutionary journey, so the material bodies that we are will forever be embraced by a God who doesn't allow even one falling sparrow to drop from his sight. But there are other ways of being, other modes of life, and it is possible that even as God sustains us body-bounded humans past our ends, we will come to be in ways we are not now able to anticipate. This is what Paul is getting at when he talks about the "spiritual bodies" of resurrected people (1 Cor. 15). Our bodies are symbols for who we are; "we" will live beyond those bodies with a God who pledges to eternally *re-member* the tragic scars our bodies have borne.

Fifth, this both is and is not a metaphorical way of speaking. *It is* because how are we to speak the unspeakable? We can only talk about death and resurrection with words that will never truly capture the totality of these events: There will always be more going on than our words. On the other hand, *it is not* because, regardless of the flaws of our language, there is a God beyond death whose fierce love for his creation means that nothing will separate the world from the God who so loves it. Even after it passes away, God will know where to find it and will, with a laugh, love it into *newness.*

God's Hope for the Future

In the opening chapter, I was critical of some traditional and popular conceptions of God's omnipotence, his power to do everything in his power to do (that is, whatever he rationally chooses to do). That Jesus, God's beloved, was murdered ought to disabuse us of a simplistic definition of omnipotence. If God was able to do it, God would surely intervene to stop, at minimum, the unjust executions of the innocent. He doesn't and so—because I find completely monstrous the alternative explanation of him choosing not to do it for the purposes of teaching us a valuable lesson about his love—I believe that means he really *cannot do everything he wishes he could*. He can, however, and in fact, he *does*, choose how to respond to these events according to his hope, which is that "all men [shall] be saved" (1 Tim. 2:4, KJV). While tragedy often evokes hopeless responses from *us*, God is a god of hope, God is *the ground* of hope, which is good news because tragedies often pull the ground out from under us.

Here, too, camp can help us make sense of God's resurrection response to Jesus's murder. Camp doesn't respond to seriousness with seriousness; it embraces the seriousness of what it's responding to even as it chooses to respond in nonserious ways.

God does this too: God chooses to respond to hopelessness with hope. Hope does not spontaneously evolve from despair; it must be *decided on*. To be sure, this—the decision to hope against hope—*is* a power. But it isn't the absolute power of a monarch; it's the humbler power of an artist, a poet, who is capable of achieving her vision even when life throws her curveballs. If we are going to talk about God's power, then we need to frame it in terms of his complete freedom to respond to the world *on his own terms*, which are terms of love and joy and faithfulness. God's power consists in his ability to moment-by-moment throw the world in quotation marks and call those things that are not as though they are.

God's omnipotence is to be found in his potential (*potens*) to turn the worst tragedy into a movement toward Easter. Like the proverbial parent who puts a frame around a child's accidental scribble on the wall, God gently and consistently reframes the evil of the universe in unexpected ways. The resurrection of Jesus confirms that God is an expert improvisational artist. He finds a way to "overaccept"[18] even the worst of the world's offers and to nevertheless lure this whole shebang to its promised future.

Reframing God's power in this way steers us clear of talking about God's plans for the future. God might have vague plans about what the future could look like, but it's more accurate to talk about God's hope. As I write this, I hear my apologist friends quoting from the book of Jeremiah, which was written in the wake of the devastating Babylonian exile. "For surely I know the plans I have for you, says the LORD, plans for your welfare and not for harm, to give you a future with hope" (29:11). But this doesn't mean God has blueprints for our future—this means God *intends* for us to have a future and for us to pursue that future *with hope*. God's "plans" for us are just like most parents' plans: He wants us to flourish and to be happy. There's no guarantee, though, which we can infer from the fact that these words were written during the Babylonian exile. As much as biblical texts want to explain this tragedy—it's a perennial human impulse—exile is proof that God doesn't always get his way. If we argue that the exile *is* God's plan, then we have to ask why, and the answer usually involves some reference to the exiled people's sins and disobedience. In other words: the exile is some sort of punishment for not doing what God wanted. But then we're just back to where we started (that is, that people disobey God; that God doesn't always get his way). Best not to start kicking the can up an eternally inclining road.

God *hopes* for the future, hopes for a world that makes good on its promise, a promise that he, to be clear, frontloaded it with when he called it into being.

The resurrection of Jesus gives me reason to hope that God will get the world he hopes for. This isn't to suggest that resurrection was always the plan. Again, as scripture is clear about, God's plans don't often turn out. Resurrection is Plan B, or perhaps an ever farther-down-the-list contingency. Resurrection is God's way of responding to the *unplanned.* But resurrection does clue us in about the kind of world that God hopes for: a world where misfortunes and injustices are righted, a world of life that lives beyond the reach of death, a world where the howl of love gets the last laugh, a world that continues into eternity to obey God's primordial call for it to come to be, to keep being, and to keep being *good.*

Leaving the Tomb with Great Fear and Joy

Resurrection begins in a tomb. Resurrection *happens* at the site of death. Resurrection takes up death into its own purposes to accomplish the unthinkable. And the unthinkable is certainly good news!

But we shouldn't forget that resurrection happens in a tomb. Which means not only is resurrection implied in crucifixion, crucifixion is also implied in resurrection.

Sometimes I'll divide my students into four different groups and ask each group to read a different

Gospel's resurrection account. I ask them to focus on key events and terms, which each group writes on the board. We then, as we often do in higher education, try to make connections. There are obviously differences in the four accounts, although many Christians, including myself, don't take this as a sign that the entire thing is fiction—*something* happened to his dead body, each Gospel account insists. Nevertheless, there are differences, and I want my students to learn that and reflect on what that might mean. I also want them to find similarities, points of overlap, and there are plenty of them. The one that always surprises them is the fear.

In Matthew, for example, the guards are afraid of the angel who rolls away the stone (28:4), the women who visit his tomb are afraid (28:5), and even after being told to calm down "they left the tomb quickly with fear and great joy" (28:8). Luke meanwhile tells us that the women were "perplexed" and "terrified" (24:4–5). Mark's account, the earliest, foregrounds the fear: "So they went out and fled from the tomb, for terror and amazement had seized them, and they said nothing to anyone, for they were afraid" (16:8). As we might expect, by the time we reach John's Gospel, the fear has been noticeably left out. The sorrow, however, is still there: Mary spends the entire time weeping (20:11, 13, 15).

What my students come to realize from these points of convergence is that resurrection comingles with fear and sorrow. Resurrection does not cancel out tears; it reframes them. It allows them simultaneously to be tears of sorrow *and joy*. "Suffering in quotation marks," as Halperin puts it. So, while I believe in the God who raised Jesus from the dead, and hope that this whole world—which includes Carl and you and me—experiences a similar resurrection, I continue to be somewhat afraid.

And I think that's OK. Even in a garden on the morning of resurrection, there is an indelible fear of the unknown.

FIVE

Hope in a World Gone Wrong

"Either love is stronger than death, or it is not."

—POPE BENEDICT XVI

"What is the event that happens in the name of God?"[1]

Jack Caputo has repeated this line so much that it has become something of a mantra to me. There is something that happens, he says, in the name of God, and this happening *is* what we mean by God. *Is*, to be sure, *God*. But this *is* is not properly an *is*. The happening of God is an event, not a thing. God is not a thing in a world of things, not even the best or highest or wisest thing in a world of things. God happens. The primary question, then, is not *What is the God that happens?* but *What happens when God happens?* and *Why does God happen the way he does?* and *How do I happen when I believe that God is happening?*

Throughout this book, we've been thinking theopoetically about not just any God, but *this God*, the God of an *of*, the God of many *ofs*, the God who comes to be in his relationship with those whom he is *of*. This is the God of Abraham, Isaac, and Jacob, the God of the psalm singers and of the orphans and widows they sing about, the God of the dead and then more-than-dead Jesus. This God, we learn from the Hebrew and Christian scriptures, which contain a good deal of theopoetics, comes to be as he arises on behalf of the world's unlucky, on behalf of all of those (a category that extends beyond humans) whose various worldings are passing away. God notices the immense suffering in the world and *happens* to it. And when we see this happening, we say: God. This happening is what the creators of Psalm 82 were trying, in the key of myth, to come to terms with—because it didn't always feel like this happening was happening the way it should've happened.

It still doesn't.

The world, as all of us feel deep down in our bones, has gone wrong, and it is this wrongness with which the Christian has to grapple.

But the world has, of course, gone right too, and we should also be mindful of this, which we call goodness. Critics of religion and theology often point to the problem of evil to dismiss ideas of God. Much of this book is my honest, critical engagement with that problem. But there is a different problem that anyone who is serious about thinking must own up to: Let's call it "the problem of *good*." Where does it come from? Why, in a world as lousy as ours, would anyone or anything turn out good? Why, in fact, would we feel a protest arise within us against evil? This protest is good: What is its source? I've been slowly making the case that this source is God himself. *Source* from the Latin *surgere*, which means "to surge or rise up." To say that God is the source of our instincts for protesting evil is to repeat the theopoetics of Psalm 82: God arises to provoke us to call on God to arise. To speak God in a world gone wrong is only possible because God makes himself hearable in this world.

Any Christian theology of hope must be clear about the world's very-goodness, about the fact that God is hearable and speakable even in a world that betrays what it hears and speaks. The evil of this world will bc annihilated, but not this world, which is, according to God's irrevocable word, very good. In the end, God will not replace an evil world with a good one, but will rid this good world of the evil that is eating away at it. The eschaton is the resurrection, not the destruction, of creation. Easter tells us that the created past, the world in its becoming, really matters, that God does not start over from scratch, that he doesn't make new things but makes things *new*. And the reason he isn't going to throw everything away and start over is because, well, he happens to like this world, thank you very much. He tried to start over once (remember our uncomfortable Flood conversation?) and realized that wasn't the way to the future. So the Creator has determined to be a Re-creator. The rainbow is his protest of both his and our despair: God will not give up on the world so we shouldn't either. There is something don't-give-up-pable, something lovable about this place. Hope for the world is not possible unless we first acknowledge that the world is *a place worth hoping for*.

Hope doesn't resolve the problem of evil. But it does problematize it—that is, it makes a problem of the problem, which is a problem of nonmeaning. Evil is not properly a thing; it is, as Augustine formulates it, parasitic on the good.[2] It has no existence in itself, but "exists" only by eating a hole in, chipping away at existence. The world's propensity to nothing is, in Paul's words, "enslavement to decay" (Rom. 8:21). Evil is nothing, *literally*. It is a void in the fabric of God's creation. The world exists by the word of God, the *logos*, which means there is *meaning* to the world. We all (sentient and otherwise) *mean* something to God, which is why we are able to find meaning in the universe. This meaning must be discovered, worked at, guessed at, formulated and reformulated, but the doctrine of creation assures us that the world *means*, and that its meaning is known to the God whose love grounds it. But is it constructed or discovered? It is constructed by being discovered; discovered by being constructed. The fact that it is constructible, that it is discoverable, means that the world *can mean*, which is a good starting place for hope.

If evil is a void, that means there is no meaning "in it" (because there is no "it" to contain anything). Evil resists meaning, is the active resisting of meaning. Evil doesn't want this world to mean what God wants it to, what God knows it can. But God resists evil's resistance of meaning, which is what I mean by God problematizing the problem. Thus: to say that God provokes us to hope is to affirm that God insists that we look for meaning; not in evil but in a world that contains evil.

Meaning and Non-meaning

There's a question we need to think about before we go any further: What is the meaning of meaning? How does meaning mean whatever it means?

There is no way to answer this question sufficiently in a few paragraphs. Scholarly books have been written on it by evolutionary biologists and cognitive scientists, and their conversations take place, so to speak, above my pay grade. But I do think it's important to briefly consider how it is that we humans—whose existence was, as we've learned from Darwin, unplanned, which means *not meant*—have evolved the ability to issue judgments about meaning, and to believe that these statements are true.

The reason this matters is because from a scientific standpoint, what we call "good" and "evil" do not always *mean* in the same way throughout the universe. It would be a heinous crime for someone to steal a baby out of its mother's arms and kill it right in front of her; we don't interpret a cheetah's actions in the same way. But does the only difference between the two events consist in how they are *read*? Is the *there* there only if it's pointed to?

In a *Zygon* article called "The Possibility of Meaning in Human Evolution," Barbara Forrest discusses meaning in an evolutionary framework. Meaning exists on a continuum, Forrest claims, "with simple intentionality on the *lower*, or evolutionarily earlier, end, semantic or symbolic (representative) meaning on the ascent toward the *higher*, or evolutionarily more recent, end, and existential meaning on the *highest*, or most recent, end."[3] For example, on the lower end of the spectrum is "meaning" that happens at the molecular level. "The presence of high blood sugar indicates, or 'means,' that insulin is needed, and the pancreas cells are accordingly stimulated to produce it."[4] At the higher end of the spectrum is the meaning my husband tries to conjure when I tell him "I'm fine" in a way that suggests I'm not fine.

What cuts across all levels, Forrest points out, is intentionality. To intend is to stretch toward (*in* + *tendere*) something, to be *about* something. We don't, of course, know what, say, amoeba are *about*, but we can imagine we do by adopting what Daniel Dennett calls the "intentional stance,"[5] which is basically a strategy for interpretation, or a hermeneutic. We act as if there are reasons a system behaves the way it does. We believe that we can ask *why?* of an organism's actions and that this question itself is meaningful. But this doesn't tell us so much about the system as it does *ourselves*—we are beings who want there to be reasons in the world for its particular worldings. Why do we do this? Building on insights by Dennett, Forrest concludes that:

> although the phenomenon of human evolution itself endows human existence with no existential meaning, it *is* the origin of the *possibility of creating* such meaning, because our

> ability to pose the question of meaning is rooted in our existence as intentional beings, and intentionality is a product of evolution.[6]

Some theologians might be tempted to say here that evolution was aiming at meaning this whole time. I don't think we can talk about it that way. But we can, and we should, ground meaning in our universe's evolutionary journey, of which we are one recent, tiny part. The fact that meaning emerges at all, the fact that at some point in our cosmic past something comes to *mean* something, tells us that the world is *mean-able*.

Evil hates a mean-able world. Evil is the enemy of meaning. Evil doesn't mean because evil doesn't intend. It is simply the act of collapse, of withdraw, of narrowing. It isn't *about* anything. It doesn't want anything. Augustine, for example, doesn't steal pears to satisfy his hunger; he steals pears to steal pears, which to him is terrifying because it demonstrates that his sinful actions aim *at nothing*.[7] Evil is, therefore, nonsensical; we can't make meaning of it.

But we can and do make meaning of the selves who experience this breach in meaning. The world means to us, and means hard, which means we go on. A question of evil, writes Caputo, doesn't "have an answer [but] it does have responses."[8] Remember our paradigm: the resurrection of Jesus. God does not answer murder, which is unanswerable. He responds to it with a word of life, a word *of meaning*—not a meaning from the past, but one from the future. Meaning lies up ahead. The resurrection is the ultimate hermeneusis, and those of us "Easter people," those of us with ears to hear, with eyes to see the quotation marks ("the cross"), follow the lead of him who calls forth what is not: meaning.

A Meanable Word

The claim that the world has gone wrong is an interpretation of cosmic history. All it means is that the world could have gone differently *and this would have been better*. Because I am a meaning-constructing/discovering human, I interpret the world's various goings-wrong and offer myself various readings to *make sense* of the universe.

There are some readings of the universe that interpret some of what we call evil—especially natural evils, like forest fires and extinctions—in different ways. Some, for instance, don't see death as a meaningless evil but as a meaningful and necessary step in the process of evolution. The world pushes on to more world through the death of this current world. Death *means* more life. When animals, including human animals, die (no matter the cause), the "stuff" of which they're composed, the resources they use up, are freed up, so to speak, to generate newer forms of life. This is clearly a correct way to see it.

But it isn't the *only* way to see it, and there are other *theological* ways to see it. We want to make sure, though, that our theology proceeds from good science. Just like we worked hard at theologizing an accidental cross, we want to work hard at theologizing a world in which the right way of going (that is, species continuance) seems to necessitate a kind of going-wrong (that is, "nature red in tooth and claw" and all that).

Here we can turn to the creative work of Pierre Teilhard de Chardin (1881–1955), the Jesuit philosopher and scientist. Trained as a paleontologist, Teilhard was one of the first Christians to do serious theology within an explicitly evolutionary framework. Creation, he says, "must no longer be understood as an instantaneous act but as a process or controlled movement of synthesis."[9] It moves from "pure multiplicity" to "perfect unity." Along the way emerges evil, or "the resistance to unification offered by the multiple."[10] Seen in this light, evil is an enemy to wholeness, which is what God's *Let there be* hopes for. "New being, launched into existence and not yet completely assimilated into unity, is a dangerous thing, bringing with it pain and oddity. For the Almighty, therefore, to create is no small matter: it is no picnic, but an adventure, a risk, a battle, to which he commits himself unreservedly."[11]

For Augustine, evil is a privation of the good; for Teilhard, it is the defiant NO to wholeness. The difference is that whereas for Augustine evil enters the world through a voluntary act of disobedience ("original sin"), for Teilhard the evil (the givenness of the not-yet-unified) is always already. We can combine both theologies to say that evil means the world is not complete, that it lacks, that it's distorted, that it might be otherwise and better. The world is unfinished. The dream that animated God's *Let there be* as it danced across the surface of the deep is still deferred. We don't know the particulars of how this dream will be fulfilled. After all, the world *worlds on* by chance and probability and luck. What the world will look like when it reaches wholeness, the perfection of its being, when it worlds the way God wants it to, is an open question because ours is an open universe.

Even scripture knows this, knows it can't say exactly what the future will bring: That is why it speaks theopoetically about the "kingdom of God" and "the Day of the Lord." Those who believe in these theopoetic promises hope for the day when God will be all in all (I Cor. 15:28). At some point, the

YES of the world and the YES of God will sound in such unity that they will explosively disappear into one another's reverberating sound waves. The two speakers (the world; God) will retain their difference, but their *meaning* will become one. What God means for the world will then be exactly what the world means for itself. God will get the world he always hoped for, which is a world that totally reflects the love that called it into being and sustains it in its becoming.

For God So Loves

There are different ways to talk about the wholeness of things, but the best way is with the word "love." The Christian tradition insists that God is love. Not that he loves but that he *is* love. God *is* what God does. God loves the world, and he is therefore *the loving* of the world. "For God so loved the world" is just a poetic way of saying that God is God.

There is something in me that insists on hoping that God is love. This insistence happens in me as a response to a call that I experience being called to me and in me and all around me. I experience myself as being summoned, being called to account, being asked to show up and laugh, to do everything I can to carry this world to its more, everything I can to ensure that the worlding being actualized in my worlding-being is a worlding-toward: toward the future, toward more, toward et cetera. Toward love. Why love? Because it is love that leads us to the future, love that sustains the beloved on her way to the future, love that lures her in the direction of actualization, in the direction of meaning.

Love is the name that we give to a particular being, which is a being-there and a being-with and a being-for. Enemies can be-with each other. Greenhouse gases also perform a type of being-with the environment. But this is a being-with that is really a being-against, a being-with that threatens the other's being on its way to becoming. To be-with another in this sense is to act in such a way that closes off a particular worlding's worlding-toward.

In contrast, the being-with that constitutes love emerges from God's desire that the world in all its particular worldings will choose to world-toward worlding. Love is God's mode of being-with the world, one that gently accompanies the world by attending to all its possibilities and luring the world toward those (yes, *those*: for there are always multiple ways of acting lovingly; love is boundlessly realizable) that are most open to the future he hopes for. God's being-with the world takes the form of a lure, which seduces the world that God-so-loves to choose to become more lovable so that he can love it even more than he ever dreamed he could. God doesn't compel; he persuades. He is "not a unilateral superpower," says Catherine Keller, but a "relational force . . . the lure to a self-organizing complexity, creating out of the chaos."[12] This, remember, is the picture that emerges from the creation accounts in Genesis: God creates out of formless chaos. His creative act consists not in—poof!—springing things into being out of nothing, but in ordering them, and ordering them in such a way that they are capable of continuing to order themselves, to bring themselves into alignment with the love that got them going and keeps them going.

Love doesn't command but invites the world to become more than what it is. God is capable of loving the world as the world, which means God loves the world in all of its worldings, both general and particular. God's love is fitting to the nature of its object; it corresponds to the particular worlding that it, at any moment, is loving. God's love for a human will be offered on terms fitting to the worlding that the human is, just as God's love for an orchid will be offered on terms appropriate to the flower's particular worlding.

Different articulations of the world need to be loved and cared for in different ways. There is, nevertheless, a consistent thematic running throughout every instance of God's loving: an unprompted, unrelenting provocation urging us on to *more.* "God so loves the world" is a scriptural way of saying that the world feels it is being invited to become more, feels that something (a thingless something) that is not reducible to "the world" is joyfully saying YES to it, is promising to always joyfully say YES to it, even until the end of time. The God in whom I hope—the event that provokes me to hope and that I name God or that gets itself named God—is a God of love, who joyfully sustains the entirety of the world at every moment by provoking it to push on in the direction of love.

Although the word "love" isn't used in Psalm 82, I do think the entire psalm is nevertheless a theopoetic reflection on the theme. In mythical terms, the psalm dramatizes the battle between the forces that provoke us to the future and those that keep us here or back there. What is it that unites orphans and widows with the poor and downtrodden? They are unsure about their futures. Women and children in the ancient world depended for their survival on their husbands, fathers, and tribes. Their futures depended on the generosity and kindness of others. If they were going to make it in the world, someone had to take responsibility for them. But in Psalm 82, nobody, human or divine, takes this responsibility.

Women lose their husbands, children lose their parents, workers lose what little they have to get by, and the world keeps right on worlding. No one hears the cries of the oppressed, the groans of the unlucky. They fall through the cracks of communities that should support them, include them, love them, the communities that are tasked with helping them make meaning. And the world keeps right on worlding. So God, who is rightly furious at this, decides to do and become what only he can. God *responds* to a world-gone-wrong, thus taking responsibility for it and giving it reason to hope for the future. God comes to be—at least, he comes to be *this God*—only as he arises to take responsibility for the world.

A Might-y God

As we've already seen, though, the theopoetics of Psalm 82 invite us to consider God's risk, which is also the world's risk. Our futures, the psalm tells us (or maybe it's a warning; poetry is not a neutral "telling"), are inextricably entangled. The future of the orphans and widows, and the future of a not-yet-arisen God, and the future of a world who calls on God to arise . . . is the same future.

But what, then, is our reason to hope for the future if God's future isn't assured? If God will suffer the same fate as our world—in other words, if there is no one to call on God to arise and therefore he stops arising—then on what grounds do we base our hope? The God that we reflect on, that we pray to, the name of God that we do theopoetics with, in whose name and for whose sake we undertake our own world-healing projects, is a particular God. He is *inflected*, *articulated* in a certain kind of way, a way that, as Christians believe, is most clearly grasped by paying attention to what Jesus is up to. God reveals himself as more than a generic deity. In fact, Psalm 82 offers a subtle but firm dismissal of generic deity: "the gods" are the ones that don't live up to their names because, well, they don't have names. God, however, does have a name, which means he can be addressed, can be called on, counted on, which means God is "this God," a being that is being-with, being-for. To put it differently: The God who reveals himself is not a *that* but a *You*. "The basic form of faith," writes Kasper, "is therefore not: 'I believe that . . .' or 'I believe something,' but rather: 'I believe you' and 'I believe in you.'"[13]

What I'm getting at is that although there might be aspects of God—the personal love that moves this world toward wholeness and hopes it gets there—that do not empty out into his *godding* on behalf of our world, it is only the God-on-behalf-of-our-world that has been revealed to us. We pray to the God of our world. Any other God . . . we just don't know about that. We only know *You.*

This is why theologians have often maintained a distinction between God in himself and God with us, between the God who gods before our world worlds, and the God who gods along with our world, who so loves our world. In traditional Catholic theology, this distinction is preserved by discussions of the economic trinity and the immanent trinity. The economic trinity refers to how God gods with our world. The immanent trinity refers to how God gods in and with himself before our world comes along and long after it explodes. Theologians have long tried to work out the relationship of these two gods—god in himself, god for us—and Karl Rahner was likely on the right path when he said that the one is the other: that who God is in himself is who God is for us.[14]

Let's remember, however, that this way of speaking is a heuristic, an algorithm. It helps us go about theological puzzles without having to crunch all the numbers. The work has already been done, been constructed. The distinction between God *in se* and God *pro nobis* is a construction, which means it can be deconstructed, and there seem to be good reasons for doing so. Catherine LaCugna and Kilian McDonnell pointed this out almost a half century ago:

> It simply is impossible to make true statements about something which is inaccessible to us, viz., the innermost life of God. This is as it should be. Not a single New Testament text speaks of God in "immanent" terms. From this we learn that our attention should be directed in trinitarian theology to the disclosure of Father, Son and Holy Spirit in history.[15]

I agree with LaCugna and McDonnell: The only God that we are aware of *godding* is the one who does so on behalf of our world. I do, nonetheless, think the immanent/economic heuristic is helpful (even if we maintain it without that language) because it points us to the reality that the "God of our world" does not exhaust God's godness. But I maintain this for different reasons than these authors. I don't mean to say that there's the God we can't access and then the God for our world. What I mean is that there's the God for our world and the God-up-there—not "up" as in the sky, but "up" as in up ahead, just beyond that hill, in the far country of the future. God is not yet the God that he *might* become, which is to say that God is not yet "all in all" (1 Cor. 15:28).

In *God—The World's Future*, Ted Peters reforms Rahner's axiom to emphasize the futurity of God's godness. If Rahner believed that the economic trinity is the immanent trinity, Peters asserts that the economic trinity *will be* the economic trinity, that who God is for our world will be God in God's fullness when the world reaches its consummation, when the world makes good on its promise.[16] I want to tweak Peters's tweaking of Rahner to say not that God will be God, but that he *might* be.

Remember: We're still in the basement.

If God might be God—that is, become the "all in all" God—then that means he might not. If God is God for our world, then what happens to God if we destroy our world (as seems to be a real possibility)? Will the God of Abraham, Isaac, and Jacob be able to get on without Abraham, Isaac, and Jacob? Will the God-who-so-loves the world continue without the world that seems to partially constitute his very being? This God is a God *of*—what if he loses anyone or anything to be of? If that happens, I believe that God will continue to god his way to the future, but he will be different. Because he will be without us. Without our world, without *his* world. He will continue to god, but it will be a different god-ing. The "God with us" part of God will not survive into the future if our world does not survive. There is a real risk, then: God might not be all that God could be, even if God continues to god beyond the worlding of our world.

The God Who Provokes Us to Hope

What happens in the name of God? The answer depends on your location. The name God might be inflected in a variety of ways throughout the cosmos. In this world, however, God is inflected as the God of the world. He has revealed himself to be the god of the orphans and widows, the god of the powerless, the god who bleeds out as a victim of state violence. I don't know exactly what it means to hope with St. Paul that God will, at some point in the future, be "all in all." But I do believe that if God is to achieve this all-in-all-ness, then he is going to need to be the sum total of all of his actual and possible inflections—including his inflection as *this* God. If even one of these don't survive, then God will not be "all in all" because he won't be the consummation of all that he could be.

Let's try a different theopoetics. In the beginning, there is God. As the universe evolves, God becomes more and more entangled with what is evolving. Once upon a time, some of the matter on a remote planet in a faraway solar system starts to interpret itself and its relation to everything else, including God. From that moment on, God becomes "God"—this God who is with us and for us and who is evolving with us. As this God evolves with us, he learns how to god in new ways. As he gods alongside jellyfish and dinosaurs and eventually humans, God learns how to god in ways that are fitting to those on whose behalf he is god-ing. God is becoming God alongside the world in its becoming. This is an open-ended process that depends almost entirely on how the universe accidentally evolves next. Whatever comes after us, God will god in new ways for and with that.

God is eternally *godding*, but the *godding* that god gods with our world will experience the same future as our world. In other words, there is a real risk that God (our God, the God that Jesus calls Father, the God we approach as You) might not "make it out" of our current climate and nuclear fiasco; but even if he doesn't, there will still be some God to continue to God on behalf of whatever and whomever comes next. A God to hold the lost material world forever in his memory and to mourn that neither he nor it has realized his dreams of wholeness, that the world will never mean to itself what it means to him, and that therefore his arising will never quite be the same.

And what of resurrection? The world and its scars will be remembered by God, and in this remembering, will be renewed, re-formed. But what this form will be, we can only imagine. The only thing the resurrected Christ convinces me of is that God will remember his wounded creation beyond its death and will one day, like Thomas, put his fingers into the world's scars and mournfully laugh. At that point, will God be all in all?

I sure hope so.

But perhaps we're reasoning in the wrong direction, writing in the wrong tense: what *will be* and so on. As we learned from the resurrection, Jesus becomes who he always was. God calls things in reverse, creates the present from the stuff of the future. Maybe hope is the clearest expression of the conviction of God's futurity: to hope is to remember what will have been the case. Our experience of time is an interpretation. God reveals himself in our timeline, to be sure, but God is free to reach his own interpretations about time. To hope is to believe that God has a different interpretation of time than I do.

So instead of hoping that God will be all in all, or that God might be all in all, perhaps true hope is to believe that God *will have always been*. Not just in the future, but even now, and even back then, in times and places where God seems to be conspicuously absent. God, writes Caputo, "is ontological indeterminacy. It has not happened yet. It depends on what will have been."[17] God's existence, his all-in-all-ness, "will only be determined after the fact."[18] God insists, provokes, calls on us, and we either respond or we don't. God comes to be as we come to respond to his insistence that we insist on his existence. If God is to arise, then we must call on him to do so. This call might be our doing, but the provocation to call on God is *not* something we thought up. We are not the source of our own provocation. God insists that we hope that God makes good on our hope. We do, however, have the power to decide whether and how we will respond to being provoked, whether and how God comes to be in the world.

Which means as much as I would like to invite you out of the basement at the end of my little book, I'm not sure I can. God might not become all in all.

Oh, but he might!

Every day, we see examples of people living their lives under the weight of God's future, responding to the forward-pull of hope, to God's insistence that they live *as if he will soon become who he has always been.* "Those who hope in Christ," writes Jürgen Moltmann, "can no longer put up with reality as it is, but begin to suffer under it, to contradict it."[19] When we hope, we are remade in the image of that for which and for whom we hope. In a world of despair, those who hope become icons of the otherwise, of the maybe, of the future whose very weight the present cannot bear.

Every day, we see people coming to the rescue of orphans and widows, helping strangers in need, smiling as they brush past one another, giving their spare change to people who ask for it. In countless ways, we see people behaving as if they belong not to another world but to another time, to God's future, a reign of love, when the world finally becomes all that God hopes it can be, and God becomes the God who has always been all-in-all.

Hope is risky, love riskier still; but the one who sustains us in love and hope is

> mightier than the thunders of many waters,
> mightier than the waves of the sea,
> the LORD on high is mighty! (Ps. 93:4, ESV)

God is the mightiest, the perhaps-iest, the maybe-ist. God is the one who out-hopes all our hopes and out-dreams all our dreams. It is *his* hope that calls forth ours when we are down on our luck, up on our cross, when we've reached our end, when our world reaches *its* end. It is God who provokes us, who instigates us, to call on him to arise on behalf of the world he so loves. And it is God who arises by descending into the world he loves, and—even lower!—into the hell who hates it.

As long as this God might come to be, as long as this God provokes me to hope that he comes to be, then I find myself being persuaded to face this world as it goes wrong, hoping against hope that it might—even now, in the event of my hoping for its future—become otherwise.

EPILOGUE

Incidental Findings

Right after I started working on this book, I got the news that no spouse wants to get: Andy might have it.

It.

The thing.

Andy had been coughing a lot, and his doctor recommended imaging on his throat. That's when they saw it.

Not that they were looking for it. They weren't supposed to be checking his thyroid. The doctor found it accidentally. It was, in their lingo, an incidental finding.

A week later, we were in the office getting a biopsy. Now, if you haven't had the pleasure of meeting Andy, let me give you some details. He's a six foot one, 215-pound former rower and things do not usually throw him off his game. But as he lay on the bed preparing for the fine needle aspiration biopsy, tears formed in his eyes. They were already in mine. (I am not, as you might have guessed, a former anything.)

"It's OK," I told him squeezing his hand. "You're going to be OK, Andy."

I could tell he was embarrassed by his tears.

Neither of us had anything particularly inspirational to say. Both of us knew this shouldn't be happening, that it shouldn't be there, that we should be out running or watching a drag show or sitting on the beach. This was not the plan!

Over and over and over, while we waited for the results of the biopsy, I pleaded with God to make it not *the thing*. Yes, I begged this God, whom I tend to believe doesn't mess with the laws of nature, to intervene and heal him.

In the end, we got the news that our terrifying finding was both incidental and insignificant. Benign. Keep watching it, they told us, but there's no reason to worry.

Thank you, God!

Or, thank you, doctors.

Or, thank you, Andy's body, for not producing the thing we feared.

I don't know whether God answered my prayer, but I believe he heard it and that he heard Andy's prayers, too, as well as the prayers of our friends and family. I also believe that God was with us when we first got the news and experienced the same terror that we did. (The Christian tradition insists that God has experienced hell. We aren't told that he was fearless about it. Maybe he was, like everyone who goes through hell, properly terrified.) Likewise, God was with us when we got the good news call and, just like our parents did, exhaled a heavy sigh of relief.

It's weird to think that we all could have deadly things growing inside our bodies without our permission or knowledge, and that unless we or a doctor randomly stumble across it, well then, lights out.

It's also weird to think that all this death happens under the watch of a God who is crazy about us. When I watched Andy cry on that exam table, I would've given anything to be able to promise him he didn't have what we were scared about. The only reason I didn't do anything was because I couldn't. I believe it's like this with God. He watches our world go wrong in real time and wishes he could do something about it.

As I've stated throughout this book, my problem with traditional ideas of omniscience is that they don't comport with our experience of love. When love can alleviate suffering, it does—but only *if* it can. Sadly, it usually can't. But what love can do, and what love always does, is *be there and feel with.* God's ability to always be emotionally caught up with us is miraculous.

Miraculous because, when you think about it, *we* are an incidental finding.

The observable universe is at least 13.8 billion years old—and expanding. Flung throughout this universe are hundreds of *billions* of galaxies, some containing up to trillions of stars. As far as we can tell, the youngest of these galaxies formed about 500 million years ago. The particular galaxy we are located in is called the Milky Way, which spans about 100,000 light years. Planet Earth is not found in the middle of this galaxy, but about two-thirds away from the center, on one of the outer spirals. The Milky Way is so massive that it takes the sun more than 200 million years to make one orbit around it. (This is known as a galactic year.) Our Milky Way is just one of more than fifty galaxies that make up what astronomers call our local group.

When we put it in cosmic perspective, neither our planet nor our galaxy holds a central place in our expanding universe. Even to call it ours seems misleading. How can we lay any claim to it? The planet we live on is one of 5,500 known planets in our galaxy. When we consider that there is about one planet per star, we can conclude that there are probably 100 billion planets in just our galaxy.

In short: We are all living and celebrating and grieving and dying in a part of the universe that nobody else would bother to care about.

But despite our insignificance, despite our triviality, despite the fact that we are, from a cosmic perspective, nothing to write home about, God has, perhaps incidentally, found us, and he insists on keeping us.

One of my Bible teachers, Peter Spitaler, taught me that when the New Testament talks about God coming to visit us like "a thief in the night," what it means to say is, "Look, God is going to quickly sneak into this world, and he only has time to take one or two things that catch his eye, so you need to live your life in such a way that *you* are the shiny, sparkly thing that God can't do without." Well, God can't do without any of it. That's what the doctrine of creation is trying to say: This world—all of it, all of us, including everything that doesn't do theology, like hummingbirds and volcanoes—has caught God's eye and now we are *his*.

My parents recently gave me my grandmother's hope chest. They had a Baltimore-area artist refinish it and he painted it with luscious blues and creams and bedazzled it with gold trim. When our friend Carol saw it in our living room, she was overjoyed because she used to have the same exact one, which we confirmed when we saw the Lane Company branding on the inside of the lid.

"What do people usually put in here?"

"Well," she said, as she ran her fingers across the cedar, "I put the kids' baptism gowns in here, and then up here on top, I put some certificates, and I think my mom's ring. Anything that's a keepsake. Some of the kids' baby blankets. You just put it right in here and that way it's safe and you know exactly where it is."

It's not very systematic to put it this way, but I like to believe that God has a hope chest, too, and that we're all in it. That's why Augustine's mother Monica can say, "There is no danger at the end of the world he will not know where to find me and raise me up."[1]

Let's hope she's right.

Acknowledgments

I've always loved doing theology. Maybe it was a survival instinct. Bad theology was being done to me and I had to find a way to not let it destroy me. So I started questioning things, questioning my religious leaders, my ex-gay therapists, my parents, wondering, along with the Serpent, "Did God really say that?" And then going further: "If God said that, did he mean it? Does he *still* mean it? Could he mean differently?"

The first real theology I read — the first real theology that reached out its hand to comfort me — was written by John D. Caputo, whom I now know as Jack. In a class on postmodernism at Liberty University, I read Jack's book *Deconstruction in a Nutshell*, which is a very brief introduction to Derrida and deconstruction. I loved the way Jack thought and wrote so I went to the local bookstore and picked up another of his books: *What Would Jesus Deconstruct?* After reading it, I began an email exchange with Jack in which we discussed theology and homosexuality. I was in conversion therapy at the time. Jack was kind to respond to all of my questions, and I sometimes wonder what would have happened to me if I hadn't picked up his book. Nearly 15 years after discovering his work, I ended up in one of his classes at Villanova. "It looks like we've come full circle," he told me as he took attendance on the first day. No living theologian has had a more profound effect than Jack has on my writing and reading — including my reading *of myself* — and I'm eternally grateful to him.

The other person at Villanova whom I can't imagine my life without is Mark Graham, my mentor. He taught the first class I took at Villanova, Catholic Theological Ethics, where he taught me the best way to think through a complicated issue: "Keep your eye on the goods." Mark has been my adviser, both unofficially and officially, throughout my time at Villanova, and has always encouraged me to focus my life and work on Jesus (which isn't something all Catholic ethicists would encourage you to do!). Whenever my career doesn't go the way I planned — which is nearly every day — Mark is there to remind me that God is crazy about me and that I should brush it off and keep going.

My theological imagination has been formed by many faculty members at Villanova, but I'm only going to mention a few more of them. Stefanie Knauss and Sr. Ilia Delio were on my dissertation board and I can't imagine having undertaken that work without their accompaniment. Some of this book comes, directly or indirectly, from that dissertation and so I would like to thank them both for helping to make this work what it is. In their distinct ways, Sr. Ilia and Stef gave me room to play, encouraged me to experiment, and assured me that the silly theology I was constructing had a place in the world, the church, and the academy.

A large part of my theology of God is based on the theopoetics of Psalm 82, which I learned to read while studying with Ethan Schwartz. I wish I'd had more time to study with him, but I'm grateful for our two semesters together. I'm also thankful for him looking over my translation of Psalm 82, which I use here. My chapter on God is largely taken from my dissertation.

This book came about as a result of an article I published in *The Christian Century* titled "Did God Intervene to Save Trump's Life?" My editors at *Century*, Jessica Mesman and Jon Mathieu, have been absolutely lovely to me in every way and I'm so happy that I have the opportunity to continue writing for this landmark Christian publication. Some parts of this book are based on some of my writing in the *Century*, especially the parts about camp and Noah's flood. I would like to thank *The Christian Century* for letting me publish work that I originally wrote for them.

After my article on the would-be Trump assassination was published, I received an email from an editor named Carl Bromley who asked if I was interested in writing a short book building out the theology of that article. Carl is the ideal editor to work with: he doesn't like long proposal processes, he's readily available, he appreciates jokes, and he's friendly. He's the kind of editor you want to go antiquing with before celebrating your vintage discoveries with a well-served cocktail. He also has a keen eye for style, which isn't something all theology editors care about. But since I care very much about the wordiness of words, I feel lucky to have had Carl shepherding this book to publication. I'm excited to see where our editorial relationship goes next.

Some of the most important people in the book-writing process are the non-book people, the people who remind you that you are more than an author, the people who take you away from your writing, who invite you to drop everything mid-sentence and go to the beach or to the arcade or to come drink a glass of bubbles. I am lucky to have more than a few of these people in my life! First up is my husband Andy, who is my favorite part of the world. He is equal parts silly and methodical. He knows how to get things done while blasting Broadway showtunes. I have a running line about being a dentist's wife, and it's no secret that such gainful employment allows me to spend time writing and reading and doing other things that don't directly contribute to the mortgage. Andy encourages me and supports me and loves me deeply. The more I open myself up to his love, the more *me* I become. I love beginning and ending my days with him. Every time I see the wedding ring he gave me, I thank God for bringing us together. And there's a good chance I'd still feel that way even if the ring weren't from Tiffany and Company. I love, love, love you, Andy.

The other people in my life who kept me going through the writing process are my parents, who believe in me so, so hard. Seriously, they have delusional levels of confidence that I will be successful. They dote on me and brag about me and, when I don't get a job or some other opportunity I applied for, are the first to tell me what idiots the hiring committee are. I love my parents and my sisters, Lauren and Bri, and I have always felt lucky that we ended up in this life together.

The biggest sources of happy distraction in my life are Shawn (my best friend) and Bennett (his son, my nephew). They live just up the street and so my days are spent going bike-riding, working out at the gym, frequenting arcades, throwing rocks in the creek, and driving a jeep onto a beach (which is an activity I've learned that straight people do). My life in Delaware would probably be a lot less fun without my two buddies and I am grateful that they, along with Leigh, have welcomed me into their family. Our local chosen family also includes Karen, Haluk, Laura, Devon, Mika and Ellie, and I'm thankful for all of them, too.

For the last year, I've had the best job in the world. Being a professor at Villanova was a profound joy, not because the institution is without its problems, but because the students are wonderful and kind and curious and thoughtful. Some of the ideas I've written about in this book were sparked by conversations with my students. I am thankful for the time I've gotten to spend with them, and I hope that they continue to ask themselves the question that Father Allan, my priest and first Augustine teacher, taught me to ask: "What does God love about me?"

This book is dedicated to Rusty, my dear friend, and to her daughters, our godchildren, Violet and Agnes. As I've written in this book, Rusty and the girls have had to endure an unimaginable loss, one which will affect them for the rest of their lives. Carl's death was devastating and it is still difficult to come to terms with. I wrote this book under the crushing weight of Carl's loss; it's being published almost a year to the day of his heart attack. There is almost no good way to make sense of suffering. All we can do is bear one another's grief, hold one another's hands, and, while acknowledging the sorrow that engulfs us, ask God for the grace to hope. I appreciate Rusty giving me permission to write about what happened. Rusty, I hope at least a few lines of this book bring you—and perhaps one day our little munchkins—some comfort.

Finally, a word on being a gay Christian. How is it, after nearly four decades of belonging to Christian institutions that dismiss my desires for love as disordered, that find ways to exclude me and shame me and pathologize me, that I still find myself being drawn to Jesus and to the God he speaks about? I suppose that is God's doing. And so I will continue to let him do it, and I will simply respond to what he does. God is love and it is love which breaks barriers and gently nudges open closed doors. I wish Christians would not enact and pursue merciless policies of bigotry and discrimination, but whether or not they continue to do so, I will continue to be a

Christian. Like Peter, I'm taken and there's no going back. I am sticking with Jesus because there is, for me, nowhere else to go. "You have the words of eternal life. And we have believed, and come to know that you are the Holy One of God" (John 6:68–69).

Endnotes

Introduction

1. Thomas Aquinas, *Summa Theologica,* trans. Fathers of the English Dominican Province (Benziger Brothers, 1911–1925), I–II q. 28, art. 2.
2. Werner G. Jeanrond, *A Theology of Love* (T & T Clark International, 2010), 2, emphasis added.
3. Jürgen Moltmann, *The Crucified God: The Cross of Christ as the Foundation and Criticism of Christian Theology*, 1st ed. (Fortress, 1993).
4. Jason A. Wyman, "Introduction," in *Constructing Constructive Theology: An Introductory Sketch* (Fortress, 2017), xxiii.
5. Quoted in Wyman, "Introduction," xx. "The system is a tight circle, in which all parts of any theology imply and necessitate logically and coherently linked doctrines around the entire circle."
6. John D. Caputo, *The Weakness of God: A Theology of the Event* (Indiana University Press, 2006).

Chapter 1

1. I know God isn't a "he" or "she." Even the rhetoric of "they" feels too essentializing. In this text, I've decided to stick with male pronouns for two primary reasons. First, preoccupation with God's pronouns is Eurocentric and academic to a point that gives me hives. Most Christians throughout the world—which is, it must be remembered, bigger than our university departments—just say "he" and that's that. Is this problematic? Sure, but so is thinking of

God as a being among beings, which is what any and all pronouns encourage. If our theology is going to be problematic, it can at least be stylish. For this reason, I remain allergic to clunky gender-neutral God talk and will therefore avoid terms like "Godself" and phrases like "God loves us and wants us to love God back for the glory of God." Second, as a gay man, I happen to really like men, and so I have no problem with using male imagery and language to discuss God. It only makes me like him more. Whatever "he" is.

2. C. S. Lewis, *Miracles*, rev. ed. (HarperOne, 2015), 150. "There comes a moment when the children who have been playing at burglars hush suddenly: was that a real footstep in the hall?"
3. *Esq*. First published in 1779. Gale Primary Sources, Eighteenth Century Collections Online, 106.
4. Thomas Aquinas, *Summa Theologica*, I, q. 14, art 9.
5. Thomas Jay Oord, *The Death of Omnipotence and Birth of Amipotence* (SacraSage Press, 2023), 6.
6. Oord, *Death of Omnipotence*, 40.
7. See Oord, *Death of Omnipotence*, chap. 2.
8. Oord, *Death of Omnipotence*, 73.
9. Ziony Zevit, *What Really Happened in the Garden of Eden?* (Yale University Press, 2013), 261. "In its own historical time it was not a story about sin—no word for sin, rebellion, disobedience, or the like occurs in it—although it does deal with the circumvention of a divine instruction. It was not a story about death or redemption. It was a story about the origins of humanity and human nature, about proper comportment, dignity, the acquisition of knowledge, and, ultimately, ethical self-awareness."
10. To take just a few examples: 1 Chronicles 12:2; Nehemiah 4:13; Job 29:20; Psalm 7:12; Psalm 11:2; Isaiah 7:24.
11. Exodus 15:3 (KJV): "The Lord is a man of war."
12. Luiz Gustavo. "How to Interpret the Sign of the קֶשֶׁת in Genesis 9?" *Die Welt Des Orients* 52, no. 1 (2022): 34.
13. Elizabeth Kolbert, *The Sixth Extinction: An Unnatural History* (Henry Holt and Co., 2014).
14. Joseph Ratzinger, *Introduction to Christianity* (Ignatius Press, 2004), 355. "What we call in substantialist language 'having a soul' we will describe in a more historical, actual language as 'being God's partner in dialogue.'"

15. Benjamin D. Sommer, *Revelation and Authority: Sinai in Jewish Scripture and Tradition* (Yale University Press, 2015), 1.

16. Benjamin D. Sommer, "Prophecy as Translation: Ancient Israelite Conceptions of the Human Factor in Prophecy," in *Bringing the Hidden to Light: The Process of Interpretation: Studies in Honor of Stephen a. Geller*, ed. Kathryn F. Kravitz, and Diane M. Sharon (Eisenbrauns, 2007), 205. Sommer's book *Revelation and Authority* is based on this earlier article.

17. Sommer, "Prophecy as Translation," 101.

18. Sommer, "Prophecy as Translation," 122.

19. Eve Kosofsky Sedgwick, "Paranoid Reading and Reparative Reading; or, You're So Paranoid, You Probably Think This Introduction Is About You," in Novel Gazing: Queer Readings in Fiction, ed. Eve Kosofsky Sedgwick (Duke University Press, 1997). "Hope, often a fracturing, even a traumatic thing to experience, is among the energies by which the reparatively positioned reader tries to organize the fragments and part-objects she encounters of creates" (146).

20. Some scholars have interpreted Jacob's struggle with an angel (Gen. 32:22–32) as a struggle of textual meaning. See John Rogerson, "Wrestling with the Angel: A Study in Historical and Literary Interpretation," in *Hermeneutics, the Bible and Literary Criticism: Studies in Literature and Religion* (Palgrave Macmillan, 1992), 131–44.

Chapter 2

1. Richard Kearney, *The God Who May Be: A Hermeneutics of Religion* (Indiana University Press, 2001), 26.

2. Kearney, *God Who May Be*, 31.

3. John D. Caputo, *The Weakness of God: A Theology of the Event* (Indiana University Press, 2006), 284.

4. John Dominic Crossan, *The Birth of Christianity: Discovering What Happened in the Years Immediately After the Execution of Jesus* (HarperOne, 1998), 575.

5. This is my own translation. I've taken some creative liberties with the last few lines to bring out what my Psalms professor described as God's "sassiness."

6. Janusz Adam Lemański, "Gods Doomed to Death: Psalm 82 as a Testimony of the Birth of Monotheism," *The Biblical Annals* 12, no. 1 (2022): 12.

7. Erich Zenger, "Psalm 82," in *Psalms 2: A Commentary on Psalms 51–100*, ed. Klaus Baltzer (Fortress Press, 2005), 337.
8. Zenger, "Psalm 82," 334. "The newly introduced series 'marginal, needy, marginal' refers to the vast majority of ancient Near Eastern and Israelite society. These are not people who have been impoverished and disempowered *by a specific misfortune* . . . ." (emphasis mine).
9. Zenger, "Psalm 82," 335.
10. Zenger, "Psalm 82," 336.
11. Jon D. Levenson, *Creation and the Persistence of Evil: The Jewish Drama of Divine Omnipotence* (Princeton University Press, 1994), 24.
12. Levenson, *Creation and the Persistence*, 139.
13. Kearney, *God Who May Be*, 38.
14. Zenger, "Psalm 82," 335.
15. Matitiahu Tsevat, "God and the Gods in Assembly: An Interpretation of Psalm 82," *Hebrew Union College Annual* 40 (1970): 134.
16. Jean-Luc Marion, *God Without Being: Hors-Texte*, 2nd ed. (University of Chicago Press, 2012).
17. C. S. Lewis, *Mere Christianity* (Touchstone, 1996), 121.
18. Wolfhart Pannenberg, *Basic Questions in Theology: Collected Essays* (Fortress Press, 2008), 232.
19. Pannenberg, *Basic Questions*, 233.
20. Walter Kasper, *The God of Jesus Christ* (New York, NY: Continuum, 2012), 94.

Chapter 3

1. Anselm, *Cur Deus Homo* (Brepols Publisher, 2010).
2. Alex von Tunzelmann, "The Passion of the Christ: Not the Gospel Truth," *The Guardian*, April 1, 2010.
3. Morna Dorothy Hooker, *Not Ashamed of the Gospel: New Testament Interpretations of the Death of Christ* (Paternoster, 1994), 9.
4. William Hart McNichols, "Catholic Artist William Hart Mcnichols on His Ministry to H.I.V./AIDS Patients," Outreach, September 9, 2022, https://outreach.faith/2022/09/catholic-artist-william-hart-mcnichols-on-his-ministry-to-h-i-v-aids-patients/.
5. James H. Cone, *The Cross and the Lynching Tree* (Orbis Books, 2011), 96.

6. Cone, *Cross*, 31.
7. Moltmann, *Crucified God*, 205.
8. Fleming Rutledge, *The Crucifixion: Understanding the Death of Jesus Christ* (William B. Eerdmans Publishing, 2015), 8.
9. Wolfhart Pannenberg, *The Apostles' Creed in Light of Today's Questions* (Wipf and Stock Publishers, 2000), 78.
10. Rutledge, *Crucifixion*, 9.
11. Rutledge, *Crucifixion*, 17.
12. Kallistos Ware, *Salvation in Christ Part 1*, video lecture, YouTube, July 3, 2015, accessed at https://www.youtube.com/watch?v=XWuu215jPh0.
13. Paula Fredriksen, *Jesus of Nazareth, King of the Jews: A Jewish Life and the Emergence of Christianity* (Vintage Books, 2000).
14. Paula Fredriksen, "Why Was Jesus Crucified, But His Followers Were Not?," *Journal for the Study of the New Testament* 29, no. 4 (2007): 418.
15. Fredriksen, "Why Was Jesus Crucified," 418.
16. Fredriksen, *Jesus of Nazareth*, 253.
17. Fredriksen, *Jesus of Nazareth*, 254.
18. Steven M. Bryan, "Review of *Jesus of Nazareth, King of the Jews: A Jewish Life and the Emergence of Christianity*, by Paula Fredriksen," *The Journal of Theological Studies* 53, no. 1 (2002): 180, 183.
19. John R. Donahue, "Review of *Jesus of Nazareth, King of the Jews: A Jewish Life and the Emergence of Christianity*, by Paula Fredriksen," *The Catholic Biblical Quarterly* 63, no. 3 (2001): 551. "The flight of the disciples and their absence at the crucifixion is open to the explanation that they actually escaped during the arrest of Jesus."
20. See Elizabeth Johnson, *Creation and the Cross: The Mercy of God for a Planet in Peril* (Orbis, 2022).
21. Council Fathers, "Decrees of the First Vatican Council," Papal Encyclicals Online, 1868, https://www.papalencyclicals.net/councils/ecum20.htm.
22. The Lion, the Witch and the Wardrobe, C.S. Lewis, pp 141-142
23. Ibid. P 163
24. Joseph Ratzinger, *Introduction to Christianity*, 281.
25. Elizabeth Johnson, "Jesus and the Cosmos: Soundings in Deep Christology," in *Incarnation: On the Scope and Depth of Christology*, ed. Niels Henrik Gregersen (Fortress Press, 2015), 145–46.

26. Johnson, "Jesus and the Cosmos," 135.

27. Ciara Reyes and Niels Henrik Gregersen, "Deep Incarnation & The Cosmos: A Conversation with Niels Henrik Gregersen," *God & Nature Magazine*, Summer 2017, https://godandnature.asa3.org/interview-deep-incarnation--the-cosmos-a-conversation-with-niels-henrik-gregersen-by-ciara-reyes--niels-henrik-gregersen.html.

28. Johnson, "Jesus and the Cosmos," 146.

29. Moltmann, *Crucified God*, 276.

30. Craig Keen, *After Crucifixion: The Promise of Theology* (Wipf and Stock, 2013), 93.

31. Jesus Edward Schillebeeckx, *Jesus: An Experiment in Christology* (New York: Seabury Press, 1979), 301-302.

32. Dietrich Bonhoeffer, *Letters and Papers from Prison* (Touchstone, 1997), 381.

33. James F. Keenan, SJ, *A History of Catholic Theological Ethics* (Paulist Press, 2022), 25.

34. John D. Caputo, *The Insistence of God: A Theology of Perhaps* (Indiana University Press, 2013), 52. "What is coming is not another world but another coming *of* the world, another worlding of the world, a coming otherwise."

Chapter 4

1. Thomas Chisolm 1923

2. James D. G. Dunn, *Jesus Remembered: Christianity in the Making* (W.B. Eerdmans, 2003), 874.

3. Jacques Derrida, *On Cosmopolitanism and Forgiveness* (Routledge, 2001), 37. Forgiveness, he writes, "only becomes possible from the moment that it appears impossible. Its history would begin, on the contrary, with the unforgivable."

4. Camp was the subject of my dissertation. Some of this section comes from that work. See Brandon Ambrosino, *Flamingos, Flirts and Flea Markets: Theo-Ethical Notes on Camp* (2024).

5. Susan Sontag, "Notes on Camp," in *A Susan Sontag Reader* (Farrar, Straus and Giroux, 2014), 104.

6. Esther Newton, *Mother Camp: Female Impersonators in America* (University of Chicago Press, 1972), 109.

7. David M. Halperin, *How to Be Gay* (Belknap Press, 2012). Halperin's brilliant work introduced me to the world of camp.

8. Robert Patrick, "Pouf Positive," in Untold Decades: Seven Comedies of Gay Romance (St. Martin's Press, 1988).
9. Patrick, "Pouf Positive," TK.
10. Halperin, *How to Be Gay*, 44.
11. Halperin, *How to Be Gay*, 186.
12. Halperin, *How to Be Gay*, 186.
13. Christopher Isherwood, *The World in the Evening: A Novel* (Farrar, Straus and Giroux, 2013), 110. "You can't camp about something you don't take seriously; you're not making fun of it; you're making fun out of it."
14. Craig Keen, personal communication, January 3, 2023.
15. Craig Keen, *After Crucifixion: The Promise of Theology* (Cascade Books, 2013), 40.
16. Simone Weil, *First and Last Notebooks*, trans. Richard Rees (Oxford University Press, 1970), 132.
17. Joseph Ratzinger, *Introduction to Christianity*, 303.
18. An improvisational actor who overaccepts an "offer" from a fellow comedian says yes to that offer and finds a way to fit it into a larger story. Samuel Wells applies improvisation to the Christian life in Samuel Wells, *Improvisation: The Drama of Christian Ethics* (Baker, 2018).

Chapter 5

1. Caputo, *Insistence of God*, 52. "Is there not an event in God? Is not God an event? Is that not what is going on in that name? Is that not what we always mean? (33)."
2. Augustine, *Confessions* (New City Press, 2023), 50. "Evil is nothing but the diminishment of the good to the point where nothing at all is left."
3. Barbara Forrest, "The Possibility of Meaning in Human Evolution," *Zygon* 35, no. 4 (2000): 864.
4. Forrest, "Possibility of Meaning," 872.
5. Daniel Clement Dennett, *The Intentional Stance* (MIT Press, 1987).
6. Forrest, "Possibility of Meaning," 863.
7. See chapter 2 in Augustine, *Confessions*.
8. John D. Caputo, *Hermeneutics: Facts and Interpretation in the Age of Information* (Pelican, 2018), 231.

9. Pierre Teilhard de Chardin, "Christology and Evolution: Suggestions for a New Theology," in *Christianity and Evolution: Reflections on Science and Religion* (Harcourt, 1974), 83.
10. Teilhard, "Christology and Evolution," 85.
11. Teilhard, "Christology and Evolution," 84–85.
12. Catherine Keller, *God and Power: Counter-Apocalyptic Journeys* (Fortress Press, 2004), 31.
13. Kasper, *God of Jesus Christ,* 121.
14. Karl Rahner, *The Trinity*, trans. J. Donceel (Crossroad, 1997), 22. "The 'economic Trinity' is the 'immanent Trinity' and the 'immanent Trinity' is the 'economic Trinity.'"
15. Catherine Mowry LaCugna, and Kilian McDonnell. "Returning from 'the Far Country': Theses for a Contemporary Trinitarian Theology," *Scottish Journal of Theology* 41, no. 2 (1988): 205.
16. Ted Peters, *God—The World's Future: Systematic Theology for a New Era* (Fortress Press, 1992).
17. John D. Caputo, *What to Believe? Twelve Brief Lessons in Radical Theology* (Columbia University Press, 2023), 150.
18. Caputo, *What to Believe?,* 143.
19. Jürgen Moltmann, *Theology of Hope: On the Ground and the Implications of a Christian Eschatology* (MinFortress Press, 1993), 21.

Epilogue

1. Saint Augustine, *The Confessions* (New York, NY: New City Press, 2023), 176.

Study Guide

Introduction:

1. What does Brandon mean when he says that although suffering is antimeaning, we can nevertheless make meaning "after the fact of suffering?" (page 7)
2. What about Brandon's life history makes him skeptical of systematic theology?
3. Brandon writes that "God is whatever God is up to." What do you think is God currently up to in the world?
4. As John Caputo likes to ask, what is the event that happens in the name of God?

Chapter 1:

1. Brandon uses the metaphor of the basement to discuss dark theological questions we don't feel

comfortable asking in the light of day. Do you think this is a helpful image? Can you think of other metaphors for doing the kind of theology Brandon is up to?

2. Brandon has negative feelings about the kind of Christian apologetics he learned at Liberty University, the kind that always aimed at letting God off the hook. What do you think about apologetics? Do you think it has a place in the Christian life? If so, what purpose should it serve?
3. On page 26 Brandon writes, "My biggest problem with omniscience isn't that it seems to be a logical impossibility, but that it seems to be an emotional possibility." Do you agree with him?
4. Brandon thinks that the flood story recounted in Genesis gives us warrant to believe that God has made mistakes. ("And the LORD *was* sorry that he made mankind." Gen. 5:6). Is this a comforting or discomforting thought? Do we have any reason to be hopeful for God's future if it's possible for him to make mistakes? How does Brandon respond to these questions?
5. There is a difference between making new things and making things new. God, claims Brandon, does the second. What's the difference between these two makings?

6. What contemporary events have you seen people theologize? Do you think these theologies have been helpful to you?

Chapter 2:

1. John Caputo, Brandon's teacher, locates him on a "verge." What is this verge? Where are you in relation to this verge? Are you with Brandon, or are you on one side or the other?
2. Brandon makes the case that Psalm 82 tells the story of how God became God. Do you think Brandon's reading is compelling? Or do you prefer to interpret the psalm in a strictly monotheistic way?
3. Why do you think God has made concern for orphans and widows a bedrock of both his and his people's identity?
4. Brandon claims that "Hope is not a spontaneous occurrence that bubbles up organically from the depths of hopelessness" (p. 77). Hope, in other words, is not natural. Do you agree?

Chapter 3:

1. Brandon claims there is a difference between the fact of the crucifixion and our interpretations of

it. Do you agree? Or do you believe that "Jesus died" and "Jesus died for our sins?" more or less say the same thing?

2. Brandon summarizes Paula Fredriksen's reconstruction of the events leading to Jesus's death. In her reading, Jesus's death comes about as the result of chance occurrences. Brandon finds this compelling both historically and theologically because it "takes the cross seriously *as a cross*" (96). What are the theological merits of an accidental cross? Do you think a crucifixion stripped of God's intentionality can still be a saving event?
3. Brandon takes up Bonhoeffer's claim that the ground of Christ's divinity is his "being there for others" and uses it to make sense of the biblical claim that Christ died *for us*. Do you find this persuasive?
4. At the end of chapter 3, Brandon reads the crucifixion within the theopoetics of Psalm 82. What are the parallels between Jesus and those whom God defends in the psalm?

Chapter 4:

1. "The answer to the question 'What kind of God would allow this devastating thing to happen?' can only be: a god of resurrection." What does

Brandon mean here? What does God's hope for resurrection have to do with his relationship to tragedy?

2. How does Brandon's interpretation of the resurrection (pages 124-125) differ from other interpretations? Does the Christian belief in the resurrection require God to intend the crucifixion?
3. What is the difference between The Cross and "The Cross"? How does Brandon use camp theory to help him make sense of the resurrection of Jesus?
4. Brandon believes that the matter of our world ultimately matters to God, and that our material bodies will be remembered by the God of life. But does this mean that we will live in resurrection with the current bodies we possess? Brandon hopes, in the vein of St. Paul, that we will be resurrected in a life that is in excess of our earth-bounded bodies. What do you think?
5. Should we talk about God's plans for the future or his *hopes* for the future?

Chapter 5:

1. What does Brandon mean when he talks about problematizing the problem of evil?

2. What does Brandon conclude from the fact that ours is a *meanable* world?
3. On pages 164-168, Brandon reflects on the biblical claim that God is love. Try to unpack what he's up to. What does it mean that love leads the beloved to the future, that love is God's mode of being-with the world, that love provokes the world toward *more*?
4. Do you believe God is, as Brandon says, the *might*-iest?